W9-AKO-935

The Art of Bond

From storyboard to screen: the creative process behind the James Bond phenomenon

LAURENT BOUZEREAU

PICTURE CAPTIONS BY
LEE PFEIFFER AND DAVE WORRALL

Abrams, New York

Library of Congress Control Number: 2006905393
ISBN-13: 978-0-8109-5488-5
ISBN-10: 0-8109-5488-5

Text copyright © 2006 Laurent Bouzereau

The right of Laurent Bouzereau to be identified as the author of this work has been asserted by him in accordance with the Copyright, Designs and Patents Act 1988.

Photography captions copyright © 2006 Dave Worrall and Lee Pfeiffer

Dave Worrall and Lee Pfeiffer have asserted their right to be identified as the co-authors of this Work in accordance with the Copyright, Designs and Patents Act 1988.

007 James Bond materials © and related James Bond Trademarks © 1962–2006 Danjaq, LLC and United Artists Corporation. All Rights Reserved.

007 and related James Bond Trademarks are trademarks of Danjaq, LLC licensed by EON Productions Limited.

DR NO © 1962 Danjaq LLC and United Artists Corporation. All rights reserved. FROM RUSSIA WITH LOVE © 1963 Danjaq LLC and United Artists Corporation. All rights reserved. GOLDFINGER © 1964 Danjaq LLC and United Artists Corporation. All rights reserved. THUNDERBALL © 1965 Danjaq LLC and United Artists Corporation. All rights reserved. YOU ONLY LIVE TWICE © 1967 Danjaq LLC and United Artists Corporation. All rights reserved. ON HER MAJESTY'S SECRET SERVICE © 1969 Danjaq LLC and United Artists Corporation. All rights reserved. DIAMONDS ARE FOREVER © 1971 Danjaq LLC and United Artists Corporation. All rights reserved. LIVE AND LET DIE © 1973 Danjaq LLC and United Artists Corporation. All rights reserved. THE MAN WITH THE GOLDEN GUN © 1974 Danjaq LLC and United Artists Corporation. All rights reserved. THE SPY WHO LOVED ME © 1977 Danjaq LLC and United Artists Corporation. All rights reserved. MOONRAKER © 1979 Danjaq LLC and United Artists Corporation. All rights reserved. FOR YOUR EYES ONLY © 1981 Danjaq LLC and United Artists Corporation. All rights reserved. OCTOPUSSY © 1983 Danjaq LLC and United Artists Corporation. All rights reserved. A VIEW TO A KILL © 1985 Danjaq LLC and United Artists Corporation. All rights reserved. THE LIVING DAYLIGHTS ©1987 Danjaq LLC and United Artists Corporation. All rights reserved. LICENCE TO KILL © 1989 Danjaq LLC and United Artists Corporation. All rights reserved. GOLDENEYE © 1995 Danjaq LLC and United Artists Corporation. All rights reserved. TOMORROW NEVER DIES © 1997 Danjaq LLC and United Artists Corporation. All rights reserved. THE WORLD IS NOT ENOUGH © 1999 Danjaq LLC and United Artists Corporation. All rights reserved. DIE ANOTHER DAY © 2002 Danjaq LLC and United Artists Corporation. All rights reserved. CASINO ROYALE © 2006 Danjaq LLC and United Artists Corporation, Columbia Pictures Industries Inc. All rights reserved.

Photograph of Steven Spielberg on p111 © Miranda Penn Turin

Design courtesy of Wherefore Art?, London
Art Direction by David Costa. Design by Nadine Levy
Picture research for Eon Productions – Meg Simmonds

The Publishers would like to thank all at Eon Productions for their invaluable support and involvement with the book, particularly Michael G. Wilson, Barbara Broccoli, David G. Wilson, David Pope, Keith Snelgrove, Anne Bennett, Jenni McMurrie, Meg Simmonds and Michael Tavares. Additional thanks to John Cork and Jay Maidment.

First published 2006 by Boxtree, an imprint of Pan Macmillan Publishers Ltd.
Published in 2006 by Abrams, an imprint of Harry N. Abrams, Inc.

All rights reserved. No portion of this book may be reproduced, stored in a retrieval system, or transmitted in any form or by any means, mechanical, electronic, photocopying, recording, or otherwise, without written permission from the publisher.

Printed and bound in England by the Bath Press
10 9 8 7 6 5 4 3 2 1

HNA
harry n. abrams, inc.
a subsidiary of La Martinière Groupe

115 West 18th Street
New York, NY 10011
www.hnabooks.com

Introduction – 5

Bond Words: the novels, the screenplays, the dialogue – 12

Bond Worlds: sets, locations, gadgets and cars – 54

Making It Real: the team, the actors, filming the action – 120

Bond Scores: the music, the songs, the title sequences – 204

Bond Takes On The World: the marketing, the release – 222

James Bond Will Return – 234

Picture Captions – 236

Introduction

Hardly a week goes by where you don't see a reference to something as being Bondian. You'll pick up a newspaper and read that so-and-so lives a Bondian existence, or someone will refer to a location as being Bondian, or will say that 'architecturally, it could be in a Bond film'. Because the movies have spanned four decades, they have covered a lot of territory. The original sets by Ken Adam were spectacular and nothing like that had ever been seen before. So, it is important to chronicle and understand the films in the context of artistic achievements. We wanted to explore the history of the movies through current interviews with our Bond collaborators and with personalities who have been influenced by Ian Fleming and by the films.

Barbara Broccoli (Producer)

When you make a movie, the public only sees the final product, they're not necessarily aware of the artistry involved. In the case of Bond, you have the originator of the novels, Ian Fleming, the screenwriters, and then all the people behind the camera: production and costume designers, directors, actors, stuntmen, title designers, composers and marketing teams. All of them have important creative ideas which contribute to the final product. This book is a unique opportunity to explore and realize how much artistry there is behind the films.

Michael G. Wilson (Screenwriter, Producer)

I got involved with the first Bond because I had done three pictures produced by Cubby Broccoli and the one immediately prior to *Dr No*, *The Trials of Oscar Wilde*, was really my first artistic official success; it was the first time critics noticed me. So, I had a very good relationship with Cubby. I knew his producing partner Harry Saltzman socially. I certainly knew director Terence Young, although we had never worked together. I was a fan of his work and he was a fan of mine. So the team on *Dr No* was a perfect match. I have to admit I was not crazy about the early draft of the script I read but I liked the people involved and I felt it would give me an opportunity to express myself.

Ken Adam (Production Designer)

It amazes me that they can still come up with new ideas for Bond, but they do! Peter Lamont, who has been involved with Bond since the early days and is still working on them, is able to invent new things with each new film. But I take my hat off to Ken Adam, who set the image for all of us who followed what he has established.

Peter Murton (Production Designer)

If you are invited to participate in a Bond movie, it is like a tribute to your own success. In my case, when I first arrived on the scene in 1969, I was first a second unit director and then an editor. I remember being on a plane to Switzerland, about to start working on *On Her Majesty's Secret Service*, and I kept pinching myself. Suddenly I felt like I had been transformed from an ordinary person to someone with a career. It was another world. And as a rule on a Bond film, we never even considered anything that had been done before. We never copied anything.

John Glen (Editor, Second Unit Director, Director)

We're always trying to be real about things. But when I created the interior sets for MI6, it was all from my imagination. I did visit the real place subsequently – all I can say is that the windows match!

Peter Lamont (Production Designer)

The success of the Bond films gave me the confidence and freedom to go off and experiment. Bond was a gift. For any film I did thereafter, I'd take the Bond attitude with me. Whether it was *Out Of Africa* or *Dances with Wolves*, which are not Bondian at all, I still used the education I got from doing the Bond scores. I learned so much from doing Bond. I learned about the placement and development of music.

John Barry (Composer)

Everybody who worked on Bond was devoted. Cubby and Harry would jump on you if you were wasteful but if the end result was worth it in their opinion, they'd say, 'Go on and spend the money until you get it right.'

Guy Hamilton (Director)

With Bond, Cubby always said that the money was on the screen.

Tom Mankiewicz (Screenwriter)

Working on Bond gave me a chance to write in the style of a pre-existing formula and hopefully to bring something to it.

Christopher Wood (Screenwriter)

Most people know who James Bond is, because the films come with an image that has been created over forty years.

Anne Bennett (Senior Vice President of Marketing)

My initial instinct when I got involved with *GoldenEye* was: 'We have to change all this, fellows, we have to change who Bond is.' And then I woke up one morning and I thought, that's ludicrous! This series has lasted a long time! Bond is loved by everyone so why change it?

Martin Campbell (Director)

There is a reason why Bond has appeal around the world. It is because he is a lone hero and everywhere, people root for him.

Bruce Feirstein (Screenwriter)

In 1962, when the first Bond came out, I was already interested in design, I was in art school studying painting and sculpting. And when I saw *Dr No*, it was the first time I noticed design in a movie and that might have been what ultimately inspired me to become a production designer.

Allan Cameron (Production Designer)

There are a lot of iconographic elements to Bond. And it's nice to think that you're contributing to the joy of the overall Bond experience.

Daniel Kleinman (Title Designer)

Although we know that James Bond will return, for two hours,
the audience has to believe that he might not, that he is really in danger.
David Arnold (Composer)

Directing a Bond film is a public event.
And I'm thrilled to have done it and to have lived through it.
Michael Apted (Director)

I'm a big fan of everyone who came before us because they've all
managed to maintain very high standards.
Robert Wade (Screenwriter)

There are some very strong images associated with Bond. There is the
James Bond silhouette, there is the gun barrel image,
there is the 007 logo – and all three immediately say James Bond.
Keith Snelgrove
(Senior Vice President of Global Business Strategy)

No matter how intellectual you are, you always go see the new Bond
film. You always give them a chance. Audiences never give up on Bond,
they'll always go see the next one.
Lee Tamahori (Director)

I was on the bus in London and I saw a dad and his daughter rush
into a theatre to see *Die Another Day*. And that made me very
happy because I realized the films still had a wide appeal.
Neal Purvis (Screenwriter)

Most people don't believe that actors are actually filmed in real environments any more. With *Casino Royale*, we went back to basics. The idea was to make the audience feel like they're part of the action.

Alexander Witt (Second Unit Director)

Making a Bond film is an enormous responsibility; you've got millions of people all over the world counting on you to deliver on their expectations and you want to make sure you don't destroy their fantasy world.

Vic Armstrong (Stunt Co-ordinator/Second Unit Director)

I worked on the first three Bond films. And at one point, there came a time where you did not have to market the films, you just had to announce them.

David Chasman (Former Executive Advertising Director/
United Artists)

The first Bond film I worked on was *The Spy Who Loved Me* and I remember the excitement of being part of doing all those amazing special effects.

Chris Corbould (Special Effects Supervisor)

It takes a big team effort to make a Bond film run smoothly. The life of one suit, for instance, can mean twenty versions of it being used simultaneously, sometimes in different parts of the world.

Lindy Hemming (Costume Designer)

To me, Bond has always been at the forefront of action films. Every new action film that comes out is based on Bond. Action films we have today exist because of Bond.

Gary Powell (Stunt Co-ordinator)

The first James Bond movie I ever saw was *Dr No*. I saw it in Arizona where I grew up, with my mother and a few friends, at a drive-in movie theatre. And I remember feeling that it was unlike anything I had ever experienced before. It was an action-mystery tale and I had never seen those two genres mixed together. And for me, it was a new flavour in movies that I had never tasted and I was suddenly craving for more.

Steven Spielberg (Film-maker)

I discovered the James Bond oeuvre because of John F. Kennedy. When he said that's what he liked reading, the entire world stopped and started buying James Bond, just as when Ronald Reagan said his favourite book was *The Hunt For Red October*, here comes Tom Clancy.

Peter Benchley (Author)

What appealed to me about Bond was his knowledge. He knew about all the things that I did not know about, but that I felt I ought to know about. He knew about cars, cigarettes, cocktails, guns. He travelled to countries where I had never been, and most importantly, he knew everything there was to know about women. As a teenager, that was the man I wanted to be.

Ken Follett (Author)

Bond is very much a fantasy figure. He may well be every man's superhero type and he appeals to people from all kinds of different cultural backgrounds.

Peter Robinson (Author)

I recognized the Bond films as a different kind of cinema. They were very attractive and designed for a very big audience. They were true to the books. The best one for me is *From Russia With Love*.

Ridley Scott (Film-maker)

I started making films on Super 8 when I was nine years old, after I saw the original *King Kong* on TV. Then I went through my big Bond period and after I saw *The Man With The Golden Gun*, I made my own Bond film. It was roughly ten minutes. I put make-up on to make myself look older and I played Bond. I wore the sort of hat that Sean Connery had in *From Russia With Love*, I had a couple of my friends playing bad guys, we even had some fight scenes... Somewhere in a box on my shelves, I still have my own ten-minute Super 8 Bond film.

Peter Jackson (Film-maker)

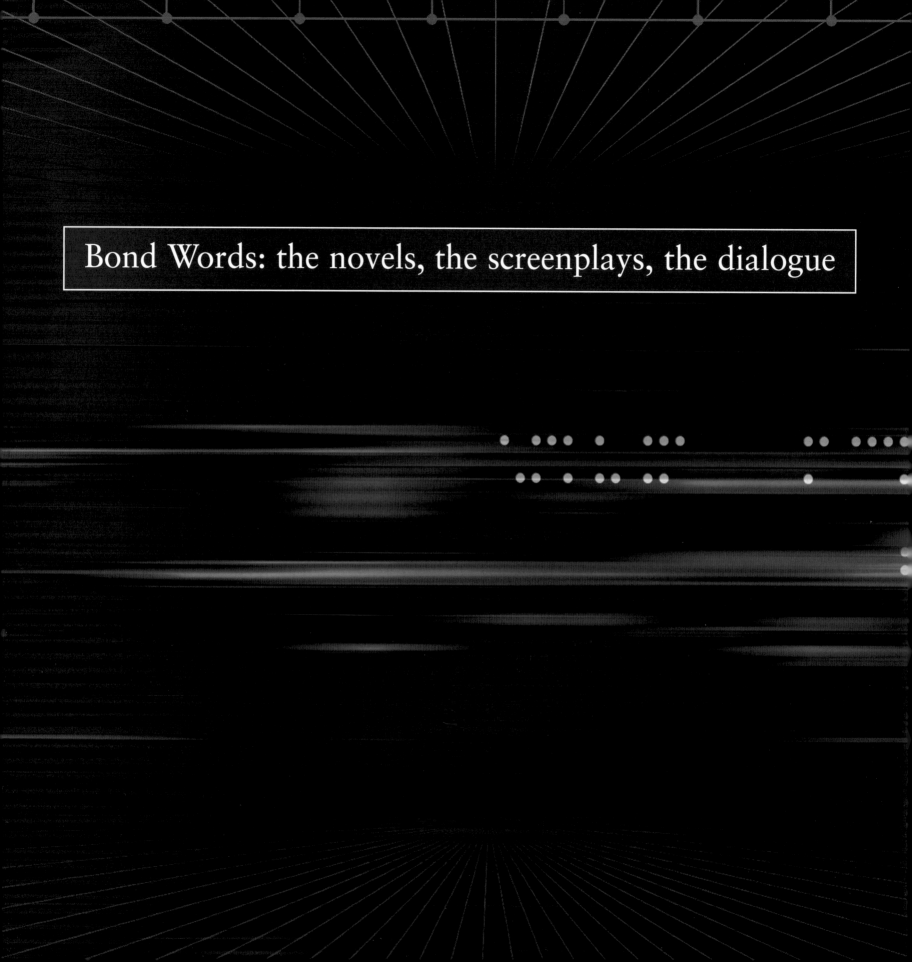

Bond Words: the novels, the screenplays, the dialogue

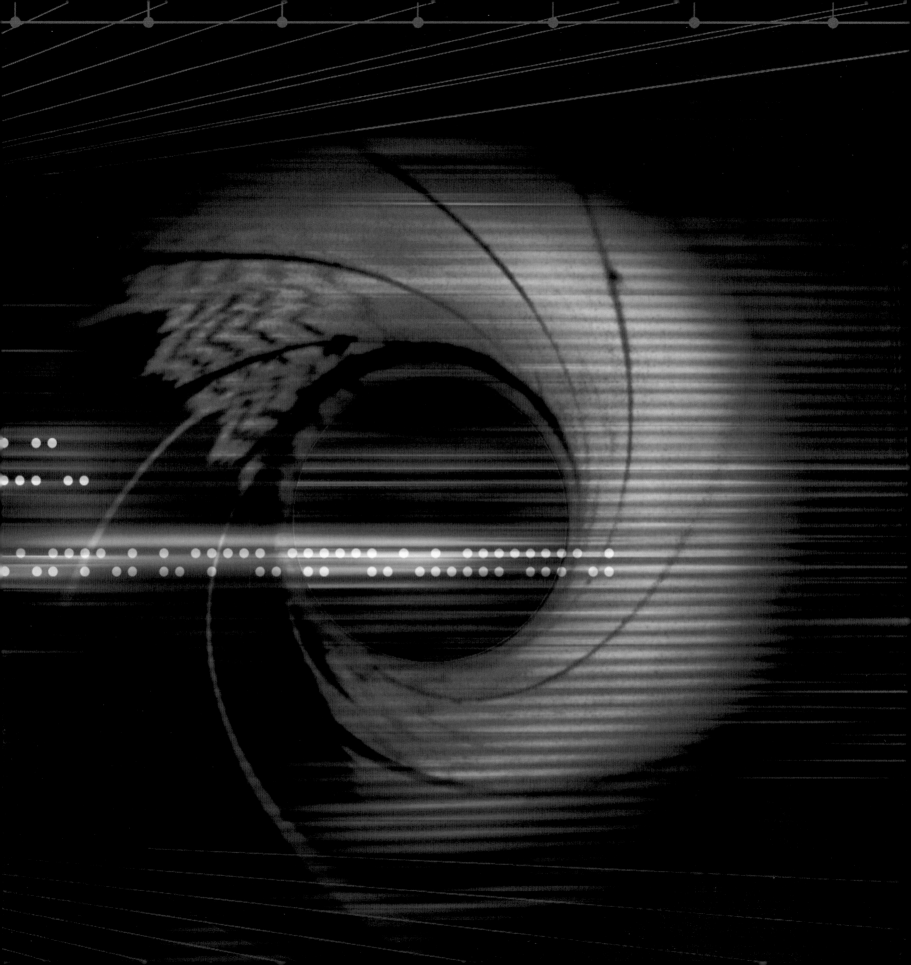

The novels by Ian Fleming were written in a visual style and Cubby always said you could almost film the books. The narrative and structure of the books were very cinematic.
MICHAEL G. WILSON

In 1961, when I was twelve years old, I read my first Bond novel. It was *Casino Royale*. The book had been out for eight years, and by then, I was old enough to discover it. And I was completely blown away. It was the greatest thing I had ever come across. It was the style; Ian Fleming was such a vivid and good writer. It was also the atmosphere he created. I did not know what a casino was when I was twelve years old. I had never met anybody who knew what a Martini was. I lived in suburban London and my parents were not the type of people who went to cocktail parties. And so, all this was completely strange to me but it was so exciting; the gambling, the spying, the money, the fighting, the women. Such an exciting world was created in those books. Fleming is the best. The spy novel is about a hundred years old and it really peaked with Ian Fleming – he was the greatest writer of the mainstream, popular spy story. Fleming said that he had been influenced by John Buchan, who was one of the early writers of this type of story, but of course Fleming brought a completely different atmosphere to the genre. It was much more liberated, much more sensual. Buchan's stories were rather like schoolboy heroics, and James Bond was a real grown-up. KEN FOLLETT

When we're working on a new film, the producers always keep going back to Ian Fleming's books. They want to keep Bond as *that* character. You put Bond in exciting and controversial situations but you never diminish him. ANNE BENNETT

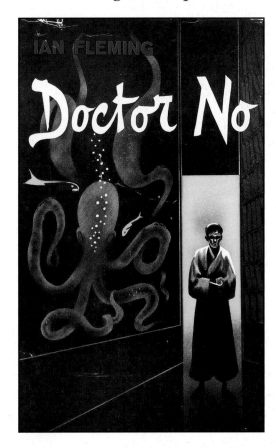

I wasn't a reader of Ian Fleming's novels. The first time I ever looked at the books was when the producers Cubby Broccoli and Harry Saltzman offered me *Dr No* but I was not in those days a Bond aficionado. KEN ADAM

I did meet Ian Fleming when he came to Pinewood to visit the set of *From Russia With Love*. He was very tall and projected a superior attitude. But he was very sweet. I had never read any of the books but I was familiar with the cartoon strips that appeared in the newspapers. That's all I knew of Bond really. JOHN BARRY

The early novels in particular read like film scripts. For instance, *Goldfinger* is one of the best books. When I read it, I just couldn't put it down, it was full of original ideas. And originality is a big part of Bond. JOHN GLEN

When I started my own career writing fiction, I wanted to give the readers the kind of excitement I got from the James Bond stories. That was a conscious decision. I felt that if I could write something half as good as a Bond novel, I would be satisfied. Once Fleming had written the first Bond novel, all the other thriller writers had to think again. So when I came along in the Seventies, Bond was a given. The hero of a thriller had to have wonderful cars, beautiful women, and fine wine. Then of course, there was also a reaction against Fleming and you got John le Carré and other authors like him who wrote downbeat spy stories. But that's being influenced by Fleming just as much as those of us who were inspired by him. KEN FOLLETT

Funnily enough, I knew Bond as a cartoon strip, in the *Daily Express*. I knew that Ian Fleming had been in the Navy during the war, because I was in the Navy as well and we had both been partly connected with intelligence matters. I met Fleming once when he came down during the shooting of *Goldfinger*, the first Bond I directed. He was not well at the time and very sadly, he passed away shortly thereafter and never saw *Goldfinger*. GUY HAMILTON

When I directed my first Bond, *For Your Eyes Only,* most of the novels had already been adapted. And we used a brilliant short story and expanded it into a full feature, by borrowing from other Fleming short stories, or from material that had not been used. We always tried to use as much of Fleming as we could. JOHN GLEN

In the books, the character of Bond is intriguing because we can actually enter his thoughts, and follow his thought process. It's strange to read the books again after seeing the movies because oftentimes, he expresses self-doubt, and sometimes he is full of self-loathing. He is a very dark character, he can be cruel and his relationship with women is quite complex. PETER ROBINSON

BIRDS of the WEST INDIES

A guide to the species of birds that inhabit the Greater Antilles, Lesser Antilles and Bahama Islands

by JAMES BOND

429 SPECIES DESCRIBED

80 birds illustrated in colour by DON R. ECKELBERRY
186 line drawings by EARL POOLE

Coming up with a name for a character in a novel is a challenge. For instance, Banks, the hero of my own book series, was the name of an old school friend of mine. I remember thinking of all kinds of other names and trying to figure out which one I should use. But Banks just sounded so right and I may well have had Bond in the back of my mind. PETER ROBINSON

Ian Fleming decided that the hero of his novels would have an ordinary name – and the story goes that he took it from a book he had on his shelves, *Birds of the West Indies,* the author of which was James Bond. KEN FOLLETT

I had read most of the novels and enjoyed them. But I revisited the books when I was asked to write the novelizations of the screenplays for *The Spy Who Loved Me* and *Moonraker*. I basically tried to replicate Fleming's style and had a sterner Bond than the one I had written in the scripts. Compared to the Bond we see on the screen, Fleming's Bond was more brutal, selfish and self-indulgent, not the more liberal, genteel chap we know from the films. CHRISTOPHER WOOD

A lot of the action scenes dreamed up by Fleming were dated and not as spectacular as they might have seemed when the novels first appeared. You had to go for something much, much larger. GUY HAMILTON

Bond is a killer. The films have made him into a killer of the right people. But what's fascinating about the books is that he'll kill anybody; if somebody is deemed to be disposable, he'll get rid of them. He's got the licence to do it and he won't be prosecuted for it. There's something very edgy about that kind of guy, and the essence of it was captured in *Dr No*, when Professor Dent thinks he has shot Bond, who is in fact hiding behind the door. They have a chat and then Bond says, that's a Smith and Wesson and you've had your six shots, and then shoots him in cold blood.

We all love *that* Bond. LEE TAMAHORI

I knew the books were good, and when I started working on the films, I re-read all of them. The novels by Ian Fleming opened a whole new world. BRUCE FEIRSTEIN

When I got the job to direct *The World Is Not Enough*, I re-read all the novels, just to get the tone and I thought they were very good. They were much better pieces of literature than I remembered. They were very crisp and had a strong story sense. MICHAEL APTED

I grew up with the Bond movies and then discovered the books. The novels were tougher and yet glamorous. In terms of Fleming's style, you can tell the topics that interested him and how he would choose to write about one specific country for instance. It's the journalistic aspect in him that comes through. It's very enjoyable and he had a lovely turn of phrase. The violence is also quite extravagant in the books. ROBERT WADE

Ian Fleming used brand names in his prose. Bond didn't just have a car, he had a Bentley and it was battleship grey. That's a very vivid and effective use of words and to Fleming, brand names were like any other words that were there for him to use for maximum effect. KEN FOLLETT

The way Fleming labelled things, and would name the brand of shirt Bond was wearing for instance, really stood out for me. It's quite a modern idea. And overall, the books feel quite grown-up. NEAL PURVIS

We're all part of the tradition of Ian Fleming.
You felt you could depend on Bond: he was resourceful,
he could handle things, he had been around,
he knew the rules. But he was human enough
to question himself occasionally. PETER ROBINSON

After I saw *Dr No*, I immediately went
to get the books. And I began to
read ahead, and realized that the
films had very little to do with the
novels. For me, the books were like
Sherlock Holmes with a gun. But the thing
about Bond is that he wasn't your typical
English gentleman. He was pretending to be
a gentleman but in fact, he was more of a
cad and an assassin. And yet, he was
working for the good team. And when I
first saw *Dr No*, I thought that was yet
another element I had never encountered in
a film before. STEVEN SPIELBERG

I'm very familiar with Ian Fleming, to the extent that my son's wedding was celebrated at Goldeneye, his house in Jamaica. There's still a writing desk and photographs of Ian Fleming sitting with a cigarette holder. But I always enjoyed both the Bond and the Saint books. I was a teenager, and the way the women were described in those days was very risqué for my generation. The characters were always very flamboyant and attractive. It was about gloss, and I used to think of the books as opening the pages of a fashion magazine... Ridley Scott

One of the reasons why the movies became successful was because they did change the books. I don't think that Bond would have become a movie phenomenon, had they kept the dark side that existed in the books. When someone buys your book to make it into a movie, they have to change it; they have to tell in pictures a story you wrote in words. And there's no possibility of a straight transfer, it's got to be changed. The other thing is that movie audiences want something much more spectacular; the book audience can be drawn into an exciting story by the characters but movie audiences want a spectacle. KEN FOLLETT

Bond is popular culture but there is no reason why popular culture and art should not go hand in hand. If you go back to Sir Arthur Conan Doyle and his Sherlock Holmes novels such as *The Hound of the Baskervilles*, that's popular fiction but I'd argue that it's also art. When you read the Bond novels, you can easily see why they appealed to movie-makers. They're not necessarily easy to adapt, but what tends to happen is that the little throwaway things in the books become part of the movies and bring about some of the most cinematic scenes. The capture of the missiles in *Thunderball* is barely in the book but it's central to the movie; you can make a spectacle out of that and the books are full of those opportunities. PETER ROBINSON

Bond Words: the screenplays

Coming up with the next script is the most challenging aspect of making a Bond film. The books were written in the Fifties when the world was very different. Every time we start with the process of developing a story, we ask ourselves the same question: what journey do we take Bond on? We also talk about how we can make the story relevant; these are not political films but we want them to feel contemporary to audiences. We look at current events and ask: what are the big issues and problems in the world? What are we frightened of? BARBARA BROCCOLI

You can't underestimate Fleming or the stamp that he put on the magic of Bond. The movies added a whole other layer of fantasy that didn't exist in the books. What made them special was that they were set in over-the-top, outrageous worlds. Broccoli and Saltzman provided a visual context to the stories created in the books, and the films are the result of a great amalgam of the imagination of Fleming and the talent of the producers and their team. PETER JACKSON

We face the same challenges as anyone else trying to make action adventure films. But it's a bit more complicated for us because we have a known character in similar situations each time. With Bond, audiences have certain expectations, and aspects of the stories have to be familiar, without being predictable. Michael G. Wilson

The Bond films have very intricate plots; in their own way and within their world, they make sense. They have bizarre characters but they all fit the landscape. And audiences accept every minute of it – but that takes writing. Tom Mankiewicz

Cubby used to say, you have to have the bumps. He'd look at the script and he'd say, where are the bumps? What he meant was, where are the bits that make the audience jump up? You have to have highs and lows. John Glen

Cubby was very intuitive about the script. He'd realize when something was wrong and would make suggestions, but he left it to the screenwriters to fix. He had great instinct on what worked and what didn't. Michael G. Wilson

Richard Maibaum (who co-wrote a total of thirteen Bond films including the first one, *Dr No)* used to say that every movie is a moral tale. That's what he always looked for in a story. He was American and a good writer, very practical and very experienced. Michael G. Wilson

Richard Maibaum had a great story sense. He knew what made Bond tick, he knew all the ingredients necessary for a Bond movie. He was old-fashioned in a lot of ways but his strong point was at plotting and structure. John Glen

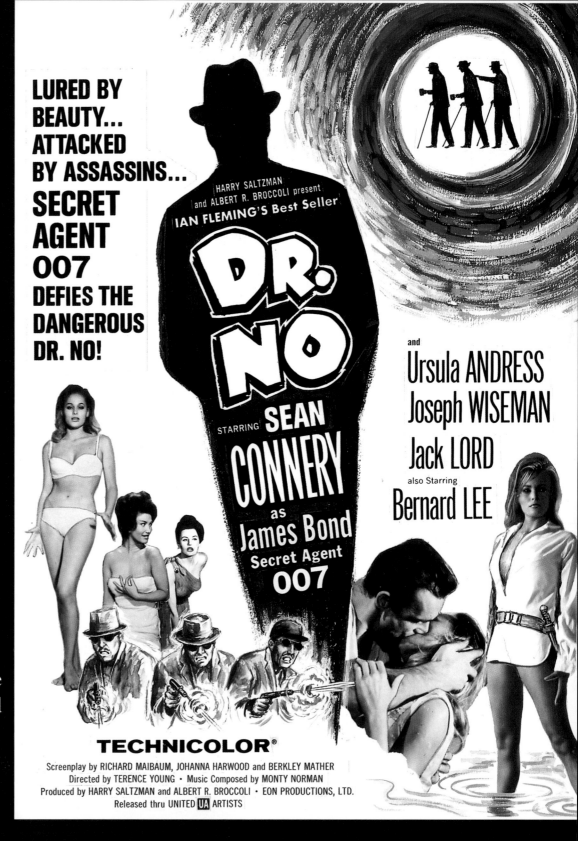

LURED BY BEAUTY... ATTACKED BY ASSASSINS... SECRET AGENT 007 DEFIES THE DANGEROUS DR. NO!

HARRY SALTZMAN and ALBERT R. BROCCOLI present

IAN FLEMING'S Best Seller

DR. NO

STARRING SEAN CONNERY as James Bond Secret Agent 007

and Ursula ANDRESS Joseph WISEMAN Jack LORD also Starring Bernard LEE

TECHNICOLOR®

Screenplay by RICHARD MAIBAUM, JOHANNA HARWOOD and BERKLEY MATHER
Directed by TERENCE YOUNG • Music Composed by MONTY NORMAN
Produced by HARRY SALTZMAN and ALBERT R. BROCCOLI • EON PRODUCTIONS, LTD.
Released thru UNITED UA ARTISTS

All of us who came after Richard Maibaum and Tom Mankiewicz got to ride on the shoulders of giants. They were incredible. BRUCE FEIRSTEIN

Suspense is an essential part of writing a Bond film. Think of the laser-beam scene in *Goldfinger*; it's a wonderful piece of suspense, with Bond tied up and the beam going up between his legs. MARTIN CAMPBELL

By the time I started working on *Goldfinger,* Richard Maibaum had produced a first-rate script. It stuck to the book but he had solved the basic problem and figured out a way to get the villains into Fort Knox. Maibaum was a great screenwriter. Paul Dehn also contributed to the script and brought out the British side of things. I was a keen golfer and therefore enjoyed the concept of the golf scene between Bond and Goldfinger. The challenge was to explain the rules of golf to the audience without being boring, because at that time, there was no Tiger Woods and golf was not particularly popular. Dick Maibaum, like Ian Fleming, was also a golfer and we used to play together. So we both had great fun writing that particular sequence. GUY HAMILTON

The first Bond I directed was *You Only Live Twice*, and we did not really use the plot from the novel; the characters of Blofeld and Tanaka were in the story, but to me, the plot read like a travelogue. And so I worked with Roald Dahl, the author of the book that inspired *Willy Wonka and the Chocolate Factory* and who would adapt *Chitty Chitty Bang Bang* a year after Bond, and we developed the script in three months. I did watch all the films that had been made up to that time and came up with fresh concepts. Dahl was perfect because he was very quirky and had off-beat ideas. What was easy in those days was that we had the field to ourselves.
Other films were already trying to imitate Bond, but they were doing it cheaply. Lewis Gilbert

Serendipity is the best word to describe how I got involved with Bond. I was just starting out, I was in my mid-twenties. I had done several musical specials on television, then I did the book of a musical on Broadway called *Georgie Girl*, based on a British film. We were nominated for six Tony Awards but closed after three nights. I came home to California, and I was very depressed. At the same time, unbeknownst to me, Cubby Broccoli was saying to David Picker, the head of United Artists at the time, that he wanted to bring in another writer, someone young, preferably an American but it had to be an American who also understood British idioms. And David Picker, as it turned out, had been one of the few to see *Georgie Girl*. So he mentioned it to Cubby, said that it had been written by Tom Mankiewicz who had to be part of the Mankiewicz family (my father was Joseph L. Mankiewicz, a writer/director/producer), and therefore had to be American, and that he remembered reading in the programme that I was very young. If David Picker had not seen one of the three performances of *Georgie Girl*, I probably would not have gotten the job. So they called my agent and I went to meet Cubby and the director Guy Hamilton, and was asked to produce the first thirty pages in two weeks. At that stage, we were not sure Sean Connery would do the film and they had John Gavin as a possible replacement. I went to work and turned in the pages. That afternoon, I got a call from Guy who simply said, keep going. I asked, another two weeks? And he replied, just keep going. The first seventy-five pages were sent to Sean and he agreed to do the film. Tom Mankiewicz

My favourite Bond is *From Russia With Love* because they did so much with so little. The biggest gadget in the film was an attaché case that blew up smoke if you opened it the wrong way. I also loved the fact that Bond discovered that Robert Shaw was a phony because he ordered red wine with fish. You could never put that in a script today. But when I was writing *Diamonds Are Forever*, I was influenced by the things I loved in *From Russia*. A good example is when Bond and Tiffany Case are on the ship at the end and the two villains Mr Kidd and Mr Wint come in, one posing as a waiter, the other as a sommelier, and I wrote that whole exchange about wine. When Mr Wint does not realize that Mouton Rothschild wine *is* a claret, Bond knows he's a fake. On *Live And Let Die*, we had discussions about elements from the book that involved Felix Leiter being tortured and fed to the sharks. Executives at United Artists were concerned about the violence and mentioned that we might want to bring back Leiter in other Bonds, so they advised us to eliminate that part of the story. Incidentally, the scene was used many years later in *Licence To Kill*. TOM MANKIEWICZ

Tom and I spent days putting Bond into what we called 'the snake-pit situation'. We'd come up with something and I'd say, Tom, how are we going to get him out of there? and Tom would say, let's talk about it tomorrow! And we would always come up with an answer. The ultimate snake-pit situation was having Bond trapped in a coffin in *Diamonds Are Forever,* or having Bond surrounded by crocodiles in *Live And Let Die...* GUY HAMILTON

Cubby had a lot of respect for everyone on the team; he was a true gentleman. I remember, when we were filming in Vegas on *Diamonds Are Forever,* Cubby would occasionally gamble at the casinos. I noticed he tipped more when he lost than when he won. I asked him why and he said, whatever happens to you in life, good or bad, first, you got to be a gent. TOM MANKIEWICZ

When I got involved with *The Spy Who Loved Me*, there were already other drafts in existence. The character of Jaws was in one of them, as well as the concept of a big tanker swallowing submarines, and those elements *had* to be in the movie. There was also a finale set in a Norwegian fjord, involving a gang of revolutionaries and that was not the Bond I was used to. So Lewis Gilbert and I sat down and talked about ideas and worked out a few things on paper. We discussed things with Cubby and Michael Wilson. I then wrote on my own, went back and discussed things with Lewis, and so on. It was like putting together a jigsaw puzzle. Cubby was always very honest. I remember his reaction when I suggested a fight on a train for *The Spy Who Loved Me*, he said, listen, we've already done that in *From Russia With Love*... And I had to really come up with something different and original to convince him it was a good idea. CHRISTOPHER WOOD

On *Octopussy*, we had a completed script and suddenly Cubby said we needed to start all over again, and we did. Cubby wanted the script to be perfect. Oftentimes, while Michael Wilson would be working on the script, I would be thinking of action scenes, which I would then have to sell to him and Cubby. One example was the idea of having Bond use a cello case as an escape for Bond and the girl in *The Living Daylights*. Everyone hated it, including Cubby. But I persisted and finally Cubby called the music department at the studio, asked to borrow a cello case and had me demonstrate how I would use it in the scene. He finally bought the idea and it worked brilliantly. JOHN GLEN

The whole idea of the plot for *The World Is Not Enough* came from Barbara. She saw on television something about Baku, the old Soviet Empire, the American and European oil industry. It was her idea to deal with that piece of contemporary history and to make a woman the centre of it. MICHAEL APTED

The fun part is to sit around with Barbara and Michael for months and months, solidifying a plot. We then do a scene-by-scene breakdown of the whole film and finally we build the script. ROBERT WADE

When we were laying out the script for *The World Is Not Enough*, we did a diagram, and you knew exactly when we had to have the action sequences. MICHAEL APTED

I think Bond films are like musicals; the action scenes are like dance numbers. And although the action scenes are organic to the plot, they're a slice of entertainment. NEAL PURVIS

We thought: *Casino Royale* is the twenty-first film and therefore, Bond comes of age. The events in the film show how he matures into the Bond that we recognize. The man that you meet at the beginning of the film is an orphan, he has been in the services, he has learned to fend for himself. His mechanism to protect himself emotionally is that he doesn't allow women into his life. The events in *Casino Royale* show him that life has a lot more to offer. By the end of the story, he realizes why he can't get involved emotionally with anyone but he also understands what he is giving up. ROBERT WADE

Cubby and Harry always wanted to do *Casino Royale* but the rights were not available. In 2000, we finally obtained the rights to make the film. MICHAEL G. WILSON

The Bond films tend to reflect the times that they're in. And I think the world today is a lot more serious. There are real threats in the world and we all feel that human beings, rather than machines, are critical to the success of our intelligence efforts. This is one of the reasons why, with *Casino Royale*, we decided to go back to what we define to be classic Bond. We went back to all the basics that made him so popular. BARBARA BROCCOLI

We've always thought, wouldn't it be great to do *Casino Royale*? NEAL PURVIS

Casino Royale was Ian Fleming's first Bond novel and it's one of the best ones because it shows Bond's vulnerabilities. What we're trying to do with the film is to go back to the roots of Ian Fleming's creation. We have in the film a number of literary references: for instance, the Martini that James Bond drinks is the same formula that he orders in the novel. It's three measures of Gordon's gin, one of vodka and half a measure of Kina Lillet. Keith Snelgrove

The script for *Casino Royale* is based on the book. We did not keep the Cold War elements but the premise remains the same. This story is about characters. It's about Bond starting out and getting his 007 status so in that sense, it's very different from any of the other films. It's a lot darker, a lot grittier. There is a horrific segment in both the book and the script where Bond is stripped naked and is tortured. It reminds me of the teeth-drilling scene from *Marathon Man*. I was so shocked reading it. It is horrendous, original and vicious. MARTIN CAMPBELL

We really wanted the script to keep the spirit of the book. There's no point doing it if you don't have the torture scene or if you don't have the line, 'The bitch is dead.' NEAL PURVIS

Humour was always an important element of the films. You can break tension with a joke and it immediately became a trademark of the series. MICHAEL G. WILSON

Some of the best lines in the entire Bond series were written by Richard Maibaum and Tom Mankiewicz. They wrote very funny dialogue and out of all the writers who contributed, they were my favourites. STEVEN SPIELBERG

The humour was set by Terence Young in the first film and it is an essential part of Bond. MARTIN CAMPBELL

The humour in the films is vital because Bond constantly faces life-and-death situations and one way to cope with fear is through humour. Bond is not a superhero. He is just expert. His humour is the way to deal with his own mortality. BARBARA BROCCOLI

I think the film-makers made the right decision to put in one-liners and wisecracks. But the function of the humour is to balance out some of the shocking and darker aspects of the stories. Like the famous exchange in *Goldfinger*: 'Do you expect me to talk?' 'No, Mr Bond, I expect you to die.' PETER ROBINSON

One of the great moments in movies is in *Dr No,* when Sean Connery is sitting in a casino with a cigarette in his mouth and says: 'Bond, James Bond.' Even in those days, at the Odeon in Leicester Square where I saw the film, the audience applauded. It had a lot to do with Connery. He looks so sophisticated, dangerous, and his delivery of that particular line basically sums up everything that one could want in James Bond. At that moment, Sean Connery grabbed the audience and basically defined the character for the screen. CHRISTOPHER WOOD

At the time of the early Bonds, I did not fully realize how great the dialogue was. I knew we had some good lines but I don't think we were aware that the dialogue would become quotable. GUY HAMILTON

In *Diamonds Are Forever*, after the girl says to Bond, 'Hi! I'm Plenty, Plenty O'Toole,' Sean added that great line, 'Named after your father perhaps.' Sean was very meticulous about the script, about his lines *and* about other people's lines. But one of my favourite lines is in *Thunderball*. Bond is dancing with Luciana Paluzzi and he sees that somebody is going to shoot him and he turns her into the path of the bullet. He sits her on a chair next to a couple and says, 'Do you mind if my friend sits this one out? She's just dead.' TOM MANKIEWICZ

The writers often come up with great one-liners. But it's not only the writers, it could be the producers, the director, the actors or anyone on the set.
MICHAEL G. WILSON

At the beginning of *Diamonds Are Forever*, there's a scene with Bond, M and Sir Donald Munger, the head of the diamond syndicate. Bond is having a glass of sherry and says, 'It's an unusually fine Solera, '51 I believe.' Cubby gave the script to his lawyer, who happened to be a wine expert and he said, 'Somebody ought to tell your screenwriter that there is no year for sherry.' As a result of this, in the movie, M says, 'There's no year for sherry, 007.' And Bond replies, 'I was referring to the original vintage on which the sherry was based, Sir. 1851. It's unmistakable.' And this wonderful moment came about because of a mistake I made. The Bond moments I remember most are the double-takes, the one-liners, the double entendres; in short, the things that you could only get away with in a Bond movie. Richard Maibaum, with whom I shared credits on *Diamonds Are Forever*, once said that I came up with one of the best puns for a Bond film. It was when diamonds are hidden with a dead body in a coffin, and Bond is with Felix Leiter; Felix searches the body and says, 'I give up, where are the diamonds?' And Bond replies, 'Alimentary my dear Leiter.' Of course, there is the reference to Sherlock Holmes and Doctor Watson, but I used 'alimentary' rather than 'elementary' because the 'alimentary canal' was where the diamonds were hidden. Cubby thought no one would get the joke. But Guy Hamilton loved it so we kept it in. And I went to see the film with Cubby at the Grauman Chinese Theatre in Los Angeles. The place was packed and Cubby and I were in the back. When the line 'Alimentary my dear Leiter' came up, only two guys sitting in the front row laughed. Cubby looked at me and said, 'Big deal, two doctors!' TOM MANKIEWICZ

Also at one point, I wanted Blofeld to say, 'As La Rochefoucault once observed Mr Bond, humility is the worst form of conceit.' I went to Yale and studied literature and I know that La Rochefoucault was a French philosopher, but Cubby thought no one would get the line. Guy liked it so we managed to keep it in the film. Later, when I got on to *Live And Let Die,* Cubby warned me and said, 'Please, none of those remarks.' I pleaded and said, 'Cubby, I saw *Diamonds* in Paris and the audience loved the La Rochefoucault line.' And he immediately pointed out that France was the only country where the film had not done any business! TOM MANKIEWICZ

When I was writing *The Spy Who Loved Me,* I knew we had to have lines like 'Bond, James Bond' or 'Shaken, not stirred', but I tried to bring a twist to them. There is a sequence where Jaws is destroying the van; Barbara Bach is at the wheel and eventually runs Jaws into a wall and says, as she looks at Bond: 'Shaken but not stirred.' One of my favourite lines that I came up with is when Bond is kissing a girl in *The Spy Who Loved Me* and she says, 'Oh James, I cannot find the words,' and he replies, 'Well, let me try and enlarge your vocabulary.' And you know exactly what he means by that, yet, it has a bit of style to it. I tried to infuse a lot of humour into the action scenes. For instance, in *The Spy Who Loved Me,* I had a truck carrying mattresses explode and a villain on a motorbike skid right into it and fly off a cliff – and Bond says: 'All those feathers and he still can't fly!' CHRISTOPHER WOOD

It's fun to put a great spin on a good old line that people are waiting for. You have to use the Bond legacy to your advantage. MICHAEL APTED

The whole concept of Jaws biting the shark at the end of *The Spy Who Loved Me* is a great example of Bond humour, where you do the opposite of what would happen in real life. I did something similar in *Licence To Kill*; since you always see planes flying over cars, we had a car go off a cliff and literally fly over an airplane. That's typical Bond humour. In that same film, when the bullets are ricocheting in the truck-chase scene at the end, they sound like they're playing the Bond Theme. But the two best laughs I ever got were in *Octopussy* when a crocodile appears and suddenly, the jaws open and we see Bond driving it, and then the jaws snap down. When we were filming, I wish I had taken a picture of Roger Moore when I told him he had to get into that crocodile vehicle and drive it. He thought it was ridiculous. But it worked. JOHN GLEN

When we finished writing *Die Another Day,* we realized we did not have the line:
'Bond, James Bond.' And so we had to find a spot for it. Neal Purvis

I loved coming up with names like Holly Goodhead in *Moonraker.* But it was Pussy Galore in *Goldfinger* that really started the tradition. Christopher Wood

A lot of the humour came from the names of certain characters. Fleming's character names in the novels raised a few eyebrows and we felt we needed to carry that into the films. Michael G. Wilson

We were always having some amusing times with the censors, especially with the double entendres and the names. They'd say, you can't say that... and my argument was that if you're worried about a child understanding the double entendres, then it is hopeless for that kid, there is no way you could protect him from anything! In truth, only adults got the jokes. Guy Hamilton

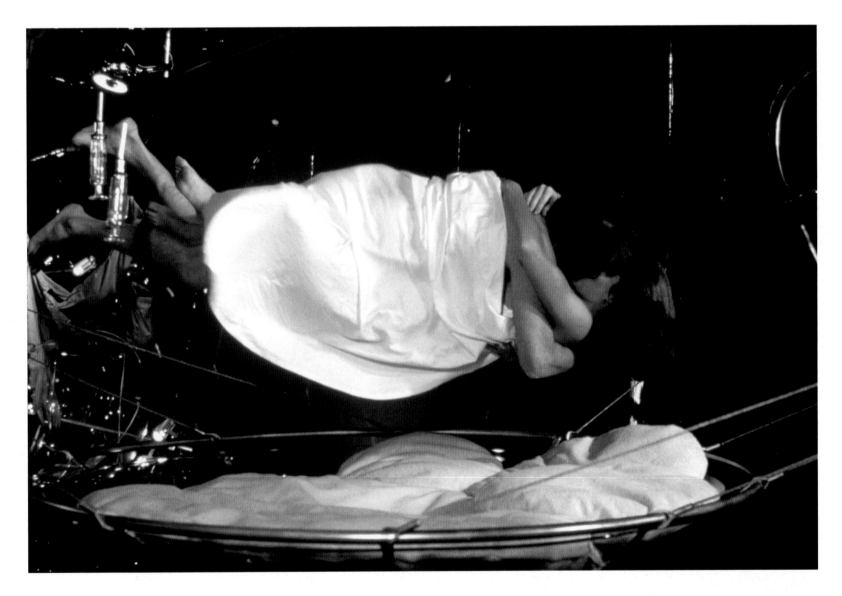

Bond Worlds: sets, locations, gadgets and cars

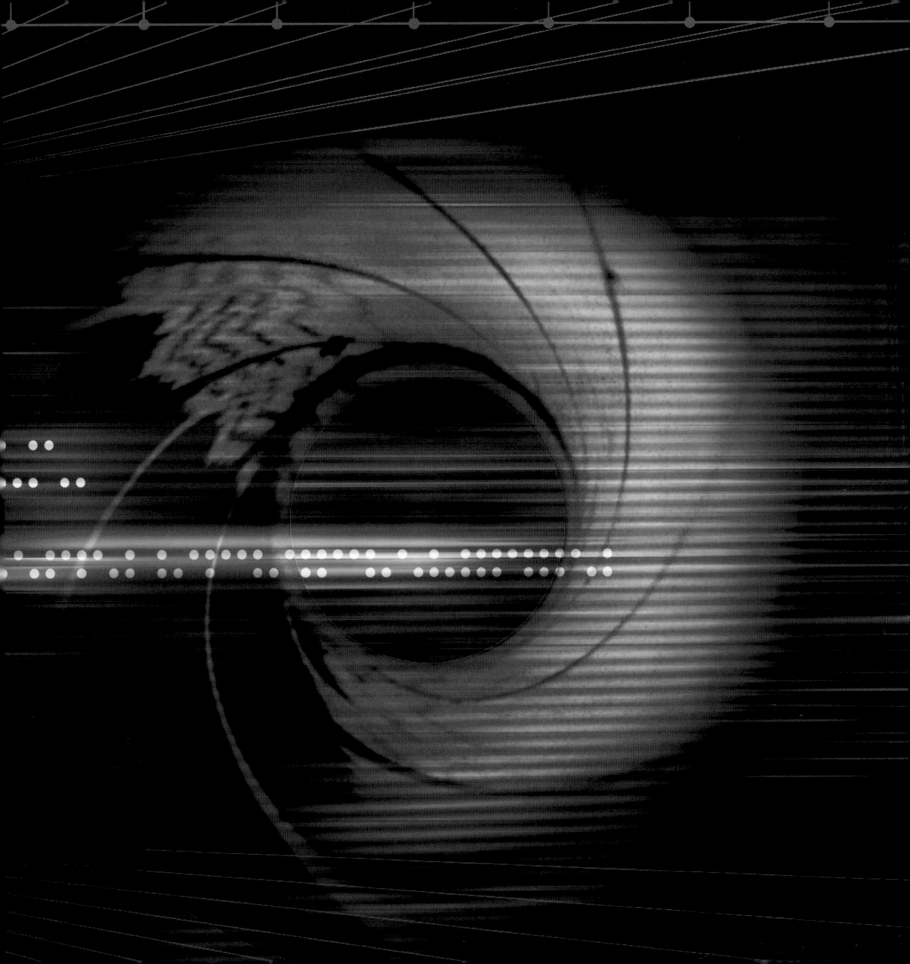

On *Dr No,* we started filming in Jamaica and I knew I could not stay there for the whole shoot because I had to get to Pinewood Studios to build the sets. Syd Cain was my art director and I had an assistant named Chris Blackwell, who was born in Jamaica and whose mother had known Ian Fleming. Before returning to London I had a twenty-minute meeting with Terence Young; he drew some plans showing me where he wanted entrances and exits, and he said, 'The design aspect of it I leave entirely up to you.' And I left. Ken Adam

Originally, the dragon tank was supposed to come out of the water. I found a tar lake, and it had a lot of dead trees around it, which I thought was rather nice. But we had to allow for the machine to come out of the water. I had to find out how deep the lake was, so Bob Simmons, who did the stunts on the film, and I stripped to our underwear and went in. It was pure mud and tar, so obviously the tank would not be able to drive through this. We were then attacked by thousands of mosquitoes, bitten all over and when we came out of the lake we were covered with leeches. That's a location I'll never forget. And in the end, the dragon never came out of the water. Syd Cain

Back at Pinewood, I decided I didn't want to use the old set construction techniques. I wanted to experiment with new material, new shapes. The fact that I had this incredible support from Ronald Udell, the construction manager, and from my art department, allowed me to be creative. It was really quite daring on my part, but I never sent any sketches out to Terence or the producers. When they returned from Jamaica, they immediately came to check out the sets. They were all pleased and I knew we were in business. The way the design for the sets evolved was quite interesting. For instance, Johanna Harwood – who was one

some piece of stolen art? And at that time, a painting by Goya had disappeared from the National Gallery. I reproduced it over night and there it is in Doctor No's living room! And that set off a very relaxed atmosphere where everybody was allowed to come up with new ideas. We had the fish tank, which was a screen with stock footage of ocean fish projected onto it. The problem was that the footage we got showed fish magnified ten times their size. So we said, the window is a giant magnifying glass. The fish tank and the rock structure of the cave gave a sinister feeling to the set, but I wanted the rest of it to be homely – and that was

Mixing up styles and materials became one of my trademarks. Doctor No was half-Chinese, half-German so his background was reflected in the design of the sets as well, especially in the bedroom where Bond and the girl are kept prisoners. Instead of real beds, we had them on platforms. We also had partitions, and sliding doors. The way I superimposed the different partitions, instead of having flat walls, had never been done before. Everything worked extremely well until the last week, when suddenly Terence said, Ken, have you thought about a place in Crab Key where Professor Dent is meeting Doctor No for the first time? I said, Terence, I have practically no money left, I don't know what to do. And that's when I came up with that big circular inclined ceiling piece, a chair and in the foreground, a table with the tarantula cage. It surprises me that Bond experts and critics alike have said that this design somehow set a style, a feeling for the next Bonds to come, because it was completely improvised. KEN ADAM

DR. NO PUMP ROOM

Dr No was the first time that I saw designs in a film that were not what I call 'neo-realist'. It was much more flamboyant, it had a theatrical aspect to it. The design was paramount to the feeling of the film, and added to the excitement of the story. It was visually stimulating. ALLAN CAMERON

On *From Russia With Love,* Pedro Armendariz was terminally ill and originally, the gypsy camp sequence was not scheduled to be filmed until later. When we found out how ill he was, the sequence was pushed forward and I had ten days to build the whole thing. It was done at Pinewood and ended up looking a bit crude but it worked. What helped was that it was a night scene. We also had a long sequence involving a train; I went to a station to look at the real thing, climbed on board and started measuring things in order to reproduce the interior at Pinewood. The train started and left the station with me on it! And I had to take a cab back. SYD CAIN

On *Goldfinger,* we shot with second unit in Florida at the Fontainebleau Hotel and at the junkyard because there was no such place in Europe. Then we went to Louisville, Kentucky to look at Fort Knox. We asked if we could go inside and we were told that it was not possible. Not even the President of the United States was allowed inside. We did talk to the guards and we took some photographs, even though we were told not to. And the few references we found indicated that the gold bars were kept on pallets. The interior, we imagined, would be very dull.

Since nobody knew what the inside of Fort Knox looked like, we decided to let our imagination run wild. GUY HAMILTON

Harry, Cubby and Guy Hamilton wanted to see my concepts for the inside of Fort Knox. Harry did not like my designs and said it looked like a prison. I explained it was supposed to; I liked the idea of the gold stacked up behind bars. The concept appealed to Guy and we went with it. To this day, people ask me how we were able to get inside Fort Knox; they can't believe it was all made up! After the movie came out, United Artists got irate letters from people saying, how could a British film unit be allowed inside Fort Knox? The exterior was indeed based on reality whereas the inside was a completely impractical invention, but the audience accepted it. On the Bond films, the public accepted the sets, they believed in them. The fact that we built the sets, rather than doing models, created the reality for the audience. Maybe it is an art form, because those sets, as simple as they were, spoke to audiences and informed them on who the characters were. KEN ADAM

For the laser beam in *Goldfinger,* I was advised by the same two Harvard scientists who had helped me with the design of the water reactor in *Dr No*. I had done a very quick sketch, I knew what the beam should look like – I imagined a futuristic gun really. They said it could work. Scientists are much more flexible than one would think. I was always prepared for people to say, 'Come on, that's science fiction.' But I always got the opposite reaction, people would say, 'Yes, this could work.' And that was incredibly stimulating. So I felt, whatever I design, someone will make it work and that gave me confidence. It also became an enormous challenge for my team, not only the art directors, but the construction teams, especially when I came up with gigantic sets. But I would always consult with structural engineers. I had Ronnie

Udell, as I said the best construction supervisor and everybody else embraced the challenge. Otherwise I could not have done it. That's when you get back to the cliché: you're only as good as your team. I still had to come up with the idea, but I needed someone to realize it. We had been to Kentucky to look at farms. Obviously, nothing like Goldfinger's living room that you see in the film existed. At first, that particular set became very emotional for me because it had to transform into a gas chamber. But I immersed myself in solving the design question of how to make all the different elements move; I decided to have the model come out of the floor, the stainless steel fireplace came down, the bar turned around. And it worked. Movement within the set kept the audience involved. Ken Adam

One day, Harry Saltzman found out about this laser beam that could shoot all the way to the moon. And I said, Harry that's terrific but who wants to send a laser beam to the moon? And then, I gave it a little bit more thought... and we figured that the laser beam could be used to melt gold; then we thought it could be used to torture Bond and finally to open the doors of Fort Knox. It was very simple really but remember that at that time, nobody had any idea what to do with a laser beam; it was just an odd thing. I'm sure scientists knew how laser beams would eventually be used, but the general public did not. GUY HAMILTON

Thunderball was definitely a new dimension because it took place above and below water, which was exciting. I started by designing the underwater crafts. The biggest design challenge was the *Disco Volante*. The concept I came up with was to have a hydrofoil with a catamaran around it. We also built a full-size bomber out of fibreglass and John Stears, our special-effects genius, made a 12-foot model of it; we staged the crash landing into the sea with the model and used the full-sized plane for the underwater sequence. But by the time I was working on *Thunderball,* I was getting a bit fed up with board rooms, so for Blofeld's headquarters I decided I would not have a table, just chairs with a gangway in the centre and each chair would have a console. Since you were not supposed to see the head of SPECTRE, I had him behind venetian blinds. In the story, one of the members of SPECTRE was electrocuted while sitting in his chair and I thought, wouldn't it be funny to have the chair disappear into the floor and come back up empty. Everyone went for it and that's what we did. KEN ADAM

⑨
INT. SPECTRE H.Q.

When I walked onto the set of the volcano in *You Only Live Twice,* I was absolutely dumbfounded. Outside, it was just a stack of scaffolding and then you walked in and you discovered this unbelievable set. VIC ARMSTRONG

Ken Adam brought big ideas to the Bond movies. And we knew what his visual ideas were before we started writing the scripts. On *You Only Live Twice* we used his sets as the basis for the story. LEWIS GILBERT

Cubby had worked for Howard Hughes and he used to tell stories of Hughes holding some of his most important conferences on the toilet. Wyllard Whyte, the character in *Diamonds Are Forever,* was partly based on Hughes and I designed this very elaborate toilet in his penthouse. I thought it would be fun if Bond, when he breaks in, lands on the toilet. For his main office room, I had large windows on one side and steps made of steel leading to a second level on the other. I kept the walls very plain but I wanted the desk to be an antique with two modern lamps and a stainless-steel circle for his safe. I also found out about this new metal with patterns in it and was able to use it for Whyte's private elevator. KEN ADAM

On *You Only Live Twice,* we went scouting for locations in Japan, and nothing really inspired us until we flew over a volcano in Kagoshima. That immediately triggered off an interesting idea: I thought, wouldn't it be interesting if Blofeld lived underneath a crater lake. I started thinking, how am I going to build that? But it stimulated me and I started sketching. Cubby looked at the sketches and asked how much it was going to cost and I had no idea. So Cubby said, 'What if I give you $1 million, would that do it?' And I said yes. Then my worries started. I started working with the art department and we built models. Then there was the issue of

lighting: how was Freddie Young, our director of photography, going to light a set that was so large? I asked him and he said he could do it and he did, using all the lights available. And we built it on the backlot of Pinewood Studios. But I have to confess that one of my favourite sets ever was Tanaka's office. At the time, I was getting more minimalist, and I got the idea of the stainless-steel chute, with Bond sliding through it and landing on a very comfortable chair. I also decided not to have normal television screens but to have spherical monitors in copper instead. None of this was realistic, it was all very intuitive. KEN ADAM

With the interior sets on *The Man With The Golden Gun*, I tried to portray our villain, Scaramanga as a very educated man with great taste. Interestingly, Scaramanga's maze was the set that gave me the most trouble. It took me weeks to figure it out. We were using mirrors, and playing with different colours, we had dark areas, and so on. I first built it as a model and got from it an idea of what the sequence was going to look like. We never had it as a complete set; instead, it was a series of little pieces of set. And each of those little pieces all worked in relation to each other but never at the same time, in one shot. It was all done in editing. In the script, the writers did a great job at describing the helium tanks – it said something like, if someone falls in them, it changes the temperature and all hell breaks loose. I'm not a scientist so I had to do research; I did not find anything specific on helium tanks, but found references to radioactive pools. Ultimately I came up with spherical shiny containers. Dry ice was used to simulate the helium. We had explosions on the real set, but most of the destruction was done using miniatures, and orchestrated by John Stears. PETER MURTON

I'd walk onto the sets created by Ken Adam, and I'd say to myself, how are we going to put all this on the screen? And that was perhaps the greatest challenge on the Bond films. But they were wonderful sets, they all worked, they were clever. LEWIS GILBERT

We kept building and having to destroy all those great sets. When I worked on *The Spy Who Loved Me*, I decided to find a way to build a structure that we could use again. There was a tank at Pinewood and by building a stage over it we were able to keep it afterwards. And that's how the 007 stage came about. What interested me specifically on *The Spy Who Loved Me* was that I used the structural elements of the stage as part of the set. In other words, I covered the structure with sheets of metal and it became the inside of a super tanker. It could house three nuclear submarines; each were about 420 feet long and two travelled on rails.

It was really quite amazing. KEN ADAM

In *The Spy Who Loved Me*, the villain, Stromberg, lives in a place called Atlantis, which can submerge under water. Cubby had heard about a contraption in Japan that had been created for an exhibition and we all went there to look at it. CHRISTOPHER WOOD

It was very dull, and looked like an oil rig. I worked for days on trying to make that design work but I threw everything away. And I decided to go in a completely different direction, and came up with this curved spider-like structure. The inspiration for it came from the work of an architect who carved houses out of rock and who used curved shapes in his designs. There is a theory that the interior should reflect the exterior. So, I did the interior sets for Atlantis in curves with one exception, Stromberg's dining room. We built this very long table and I had a very good scenic painter do reproductions of my favourite Renaissance tapestries. And at one point, all the tapestries went up as Atlantis was rising to the surface. There is no doubt that Atlantis was for me an explosion of ideas. KEN ADAM

Moonraker was meant to premiere in the week of the space shuttle's take-off into space. Unfortunately, they had engine trouble which put the programme back two years. So instead of being science fact, it was science fiction. PETER LAMONT

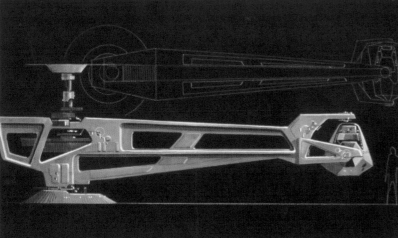

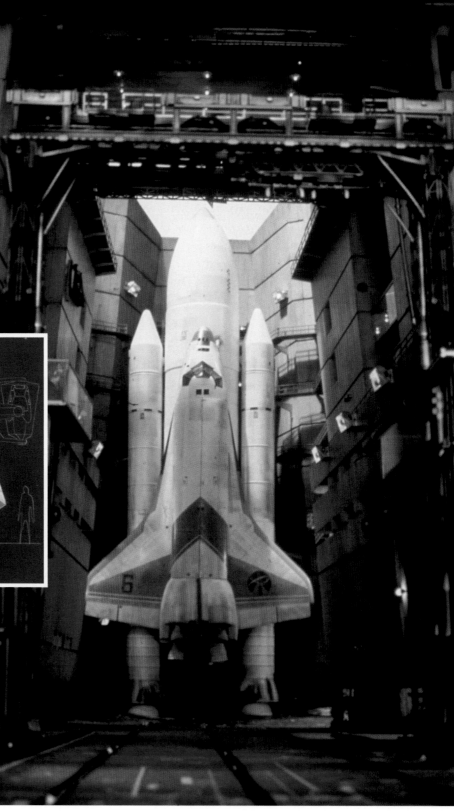

Moonraker was for me the most complicated Bond of all. I felt I had to do a lot of research; I didn't want science-fiction, I wanted science fact. Before I started working on the space station for instance, I went to NASA and they showed me their latest design; it was a series of cylinders bolted together with solar panels. I particularly liked the idea of the cylinders and decided to have the space station look like a mobile. Each arm, each cylinder had a different length and as it started rotating, you kept getting a different look depending on the angle. For the inside of the space station, I had in all my sketches, even the early ones, a giant telescope as the focal point of the set. I created several levels and incorporated tubes to give the impression of a city in space. Some of the tubes were for people to walk through, others were used to launch the spherical pods. But my favourite set on *Moonraker* was what I called the exhaust chamber. It was supposed to be underneath the rocket of the Moonraker. In reality, you would have a pit where the flames go in during take off. But I made it a conference room, with a circular table and chairs that would fold, and flatten into the ground. I did a sketch for the centrifuge set, based on something similar I had seen in America. Derek Meddings saw the final sketches and said, brilliant, I'll do it as a model. But I told him I wanted to build it for real and found someone in France who could do it. The only problem was that we could not rotate it very fast, so for the shots where it's going full-speed, Derek got to build his model. But it was a very effective set. On the film, we used all of the three big studios in France. At times, we had three or four units working in different parts of the world, including Derek Meddings and Peter Lamont supervising the miniature work and the space battle. So it was a logistical nightmare. We also staged our own carnival in Rio. I had reserved some of the schools who make the costumes and the floats and we had our own carnival three months after the official one had happened. KEN ADAM

"MOONRAKER" INT. SHUTTLE LAUNCH COMPLEX

Peter Lamont was a great asset to me on all the Bond films I directed. He always knew what would work for the audience. I remember he came up with the idea of making Octopussy's bed in the shape of an octopus. I thought the audience would never quite notice it but on the contrary, it got a great laugh. When we got to *A View To A Kill*, the 007 stage had burned down to the ground during the filming of Ridley Scott's *Legend*. And it was Peter who took on the challenge of rebuilding it and he then designed the most amazing set for the mine; it was truly extraordinary. JOHN GLEN

When I was in London scoring *Return of the King*, I called and got a tour of Pinewood Studios. I saw the 007 stage but the most exciting part was to visit the garden where the beginning of *From Russia With Love* takes place, and to see the alleyway where the chase with the Aston Martin in *Goldfinger* was filmed. PETER JACKSON

I only ever got close to Cubby Broccoli the day the 007 stage burned down. I was doing my movie *Legend* and one lunchtime I was in the editing room and somebody charged in saying the Bond stage was on fire. And I said, come on, get out of here, and he said no, no seriously you must come now. So I ran over there. Helicopters were circling and I saw this fireman standing there scratching his head. There was a person standing behind me, I turned around and it was Cubby. He looked at me and I looked at him and I said, I'm really sorry, and I walked off. RIDLEY SCOTT

For *GoldenEye* we filmed at Leavesden,
which used to be a Rolls Royce factory.
We converted the facility into five soundstages and also
shot some of the exterior scenes there,
such as portions of the tank chase. PETER LAMONT

At the time of *GoldenEye,* Pinewood was booked up. In fact all of the studios were booked up. So we went looking for warehouses, and we decided on Leavesden. I worked closely with Peter Lamont, who is a fantastic production designer, and nothing is too much trouble for him, he is extremely helpful and efficient. He is amazingly flexible, but he also has very strong views. One of my favourite sets on the film is the statue graveyard, where Bond has a confrontation with the villain. That was a Peter Lamont special. MARTIN CAMPBELL

We were originally going to film the entire tank chase in St Petersburg. But we got into a crunch, and we decided to send second unit to do some of the shots on location. We also built the city as a set at Leavesden Studios. The decision allowed us to freely choreograph a great action scene and watching the film, you cannot tell it was done on a set. MARTIN CAMPBELL

For *Tomorrow Never Dies,* originally, we were going to build the sets at Leavesden, where *GoldenEye* had been done. In the end, Tony Wade, my art director, found an industrial space which had been built for the aircraft industry and turned into a warehouse for groceries, and it was empty at the time. It was not in good condition but what was great from my point of view, was that there was an old runway – by then we knew we would have to build a street complex, and the runway was absolutely perfect for it. So we went ahead and turned it into a proper studio. We built the interior of the stealth ship on the 007 set and the tank at Pinewood. For the stealth ship, we first looked at American technology and we then created some terrific designs – in the end, we streamlined the shape to something that was less fantastical, and more realistic. The exterior of the ship was a combination of miniature and CGI. I was particularly pleased with the interior design, which we built on a set at Pinewood. We had trap doors, the cutting machine and so on, and I really hope I managed to convey the spirit of the earlier Bond films with that particular set. I loved the scale of it and it was a fun thing to do. The chainsaw-type weapon that slices through the belly of a ship was based on existing cutting machinery that is used in the oil and diamond industries, as well as technology that was used to dig the channel tunnel. The machine had to perform a lot of different actions, including killing the villain. So I collaborated with Chris Corbould and his special effects team on it. There were about three different versions of it; one with real blades that could not go under water, one that could go in water and one with extremely soft foam blades that you could put very close to people.

I loved the idea of Wai Lin's dirty old bicycle shop. It was a small set but I loved designing it. It was supposed to be a bit tongue-in-cheek. The geography of it was dictated by the fight that went on in the earlier part of the sequence. And then I loved the fact that we had a complete textural change from this dirty shop into this ultra-modern, high-tech control room. When the set transforms, there was absolutely nothing mechanical about it. It was exclusively manpowered, controlled by grips pushing things around on cue. That's a lot more reliable than something that would be radio-controlled – it allows the director to ask for things to be revealed faster or slower. There's no hydraulic leaking or crossed wires. On the film, half the 007 stage at Pinewoood was used for the interior of the stealth ship. The rest was for the British sunken ship. The challenge was that we needed a tank that was 16 feet deep and the 007 tank is only 8 feet deep. So we actually built up steel walls to extend it. It was very complicated because the water had to be chlorinated, it had to be at an acceptable temperature for the actors, we had to use special paint that would not peel off. We did many experiments to get this right. ALLAN CAMERON

For Carver's huge video wall, the hardest thing was to create believable and realistic images on the screens. One of the things that can take an audience out of a movie is if the signage on shops or newspaper headlines seem to have been generated by a graphic artist. We had a great team creating all the images you see on the video screens and we would test them, film them and our director Roger Spottiswoode would make changes until we felt the look was realistic. It was a long process and that was the challenge of that particular set. ALLAN CAMERON

On *The World Is Not Enough*, I always had a little voice inside my head saying, pay attention to all the details. For example, the submarine set: I did not have to shoot it until June and they started building it in November. Normally, I'd say, I don't need to worry about this for a few months but I did. So I paid a lot of attention to the rhythm of designing, and building set after set after set. One of my favourite sequences in the film took place in the caviar factory. It's one of those occasions where the story evolved around the set. We brought in the helicopter with the dangling swords and we sliced up the set! MICHAEL APTED

It required a massive rig and we were able to get a tower crane which is the biggest crane in Europe. All the movements were programmed into a computer, so we could plan out exactly what we wanted it to do. The amazing thing was that everything you see was mainly done for real. And traditionally with Bond, you always try to do things on camera. CHRIS CORBOULD

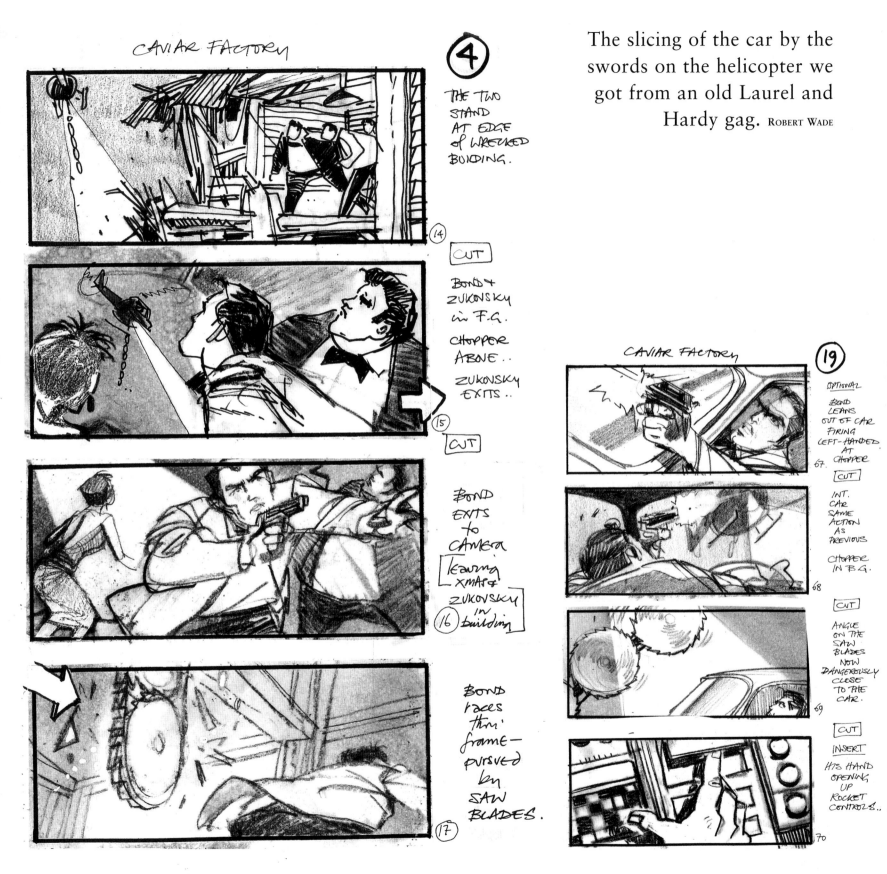

CAVIAR FACTORY

④

THE TWO STAND AT EDGE OF WRECKED BUILDING.

14

CUT

BOND + ZUKOVSKY in F.G.

CHOPPER ABOVE..

ZUKOVSKY EXITS..

15

CUT

BOND EXITS to CAMERA [leaving XMAS + ZUKOVSKY in building] 16

BOND races thru' frame - pursued by SAW BLADES. 17

The slicing of the car by the swords on the helicopter we got from an old Laurel and Hardy gag. ROBERT WADE

CAVIAR FACTORY ⑲

OPTIONAL BOND LEANS OUT OF CAR FIRING LEFT-HANDED AT CHOPPER 67

CUT

INT. CAR SAME ACTION AS PREVIOUS

CHOPPER IN B.G. 68

CUT

ANGLE ON THE SAW BLADES NOW DANGEROUSLY CLOSE TO THE CAR. 69

CUT

INSERT HIS HAND OPENING UP ROCKET CONTROLS.. 70

We were writing *Die Another Day* and Barbara Broccoli mentioned she had read about an ice palace, located somewhere in Sweden. And she said, wouldn't it be a great place for a villain and we quite liked that. ROBERT WADE

I went and stayed at the real place in Sweden. They bring in a new architect every summer and build it when the weather gets cold. Everything is done in ice. And that was the basis for the design of the Ice Palace, which we built at Pinewood Studios. PETER LAMONT

In the script, the Ice Palace was just a place where Bond stays. There were no real action sequences involving that set. We built it on the 007 stage, and we were spending so much time and money creating this awesome place that I felt we needed to do something with it. We had a car chase on ice outside the palace, and one week into building it, I went to Peter Lamont and asked, what if we do part of the car chase inside the palace? I explained that I needed to know what was involved with modifying the set so it could sustain a car chase. And Peter said, let me think about it overnight. The next day, I suggested the idea to Barbara and Michael and they simply said, that's great. Peter Lamont explained what the implications were and they went along with it. That's the thing about Bond films that separates them from other pictures; they could see it was a good idea and that's what mattered to them. We must have been eight weeks into the film and all of us were still trying to figure out where the climactic confrontation between Bond and the villain should take place. I did not want another underground cave. There was this idea of a fake beach, and then one morning I thought, let's go airborne and have the sequence in a giant plane. It was a challenging idea because we had to build the set very fast, but Peter Lamont pulled it off. LEE TAMAHORI

In *Casino Royale*, we have a scene in M's house. What sort of house do you imagine her living in? That's a very interesting question. Is it an old, classic house? No… I said, it's very modern. It's the opposite of what you'd expect. This woman is full of surprises. She is also very sophisticated. So we've gone for something modern. MARTIN CAMPBELL

We built about fifty sets on *Casino Royale*, including M's penthouse, the interior of the salon privé at the Casino Royale, the interior of the barge where Bond is tortured, the interior of Le Chiffre's yacht… Most of the sets were done in the Czech Republic at Barrendov Film Studios. We also recreated the famous Body Worlds exhibit at the Science Centre where Dimitrios is killed. For that particular set, we got the full cooperation of the exhibit's creator Gunther Von Harven. We also had the amazing sinking house on the 007 set at Pinewood Studios. We built two separate houses, one that could sink up to one level, another that could go down further. PETER LAMONT

As is customary on Bond films, the set gets destroyed at the end. On *Tomorrow Never Dies*, Chris Corbould, our special effects man, warned me that the big explosion was going to be enormous. So, I went outside and it was indeed extraordinary! And there goes the set. ALLAN CAMERON

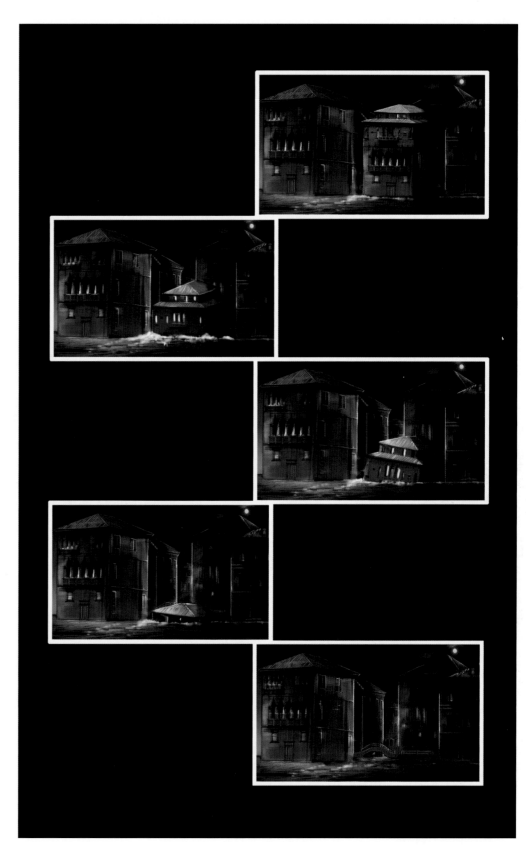

In one of the novels, Fleming describes Bond on a transatlantic flight and that was unusual because few people travelled in those days. He allowed readers to live what seemed like the future. By reading Bond, you could live a life you could only dream of. PETER ROBINSON

I used to scout locations and film with a 16mm camera. On *Thunderball*, I found a big villa with two pools in the Bahamas. I got in touch with the people who owned it and that triggered the idea of using a real location for Largo's place, with the pool for the sharks. KEN ADAM

Bond Worlds: the locations

Because we work with many of the same people all the time, they're pretty well indoctrinated into what is appropriate for a Bond movie. So, someone like Peter Lamont will say, 'I saw this building or that design when I was on vacation...' and we will discuss the idea with the director and if we all like it, we'll incorporate it in the story. BARBARA BROCCOLI

One thing that was very much part of Bond for Harry and Cubby, was exotic locations. There are a lot of reasons for this; one of them is that at the time, there were no package holidays. Flying was very expensive and with the films, we promised to take you to the most glorious places, places you've never been to in your lives, places you were not likely to ever go to. Location scouting was great fun. And that's where I did half my directing. GUY HAMILTON

91

When I got involved with designing the sets for *On Her Majesty's Secret Service,* Harry Saltzman came to me and said, I've found the ideal spot for Blofeld. That afternoon, he booked a plane and we went to a place that had been built before World War II and was located on the German border; it was an underground facility, with guns pointed towards the border. It was closed to the public, but mention Bond and you can get in anywhere. Then Harry took me to the Swiss border to another defence area built inside a mountain. Frankly, I was not crazy about either location, and rather than going underground, I thought we should go up. That's when I suggested a place that faced the Eiger mountain. They were starting to build a restaurant and I thought it would be perfect timing to get in there before they finished it. The Swiss government was not crazy about the idea of having us there until I explained that I would build a heliport as part of the set, which they could then keep and use for mountain rescue operations. The heliport had to withstand winds going 120 miles an hour as well as snow pressure, and we had to bring in Italian engineers who had built the Simplon tunnel. The cable cars had to be completed so that we could use them. I built the interior of the cable car machine room back at Pinewood Studios; the large wheels were made out of wood and painted to look like metal. But the main dining area, the Alpine room, was done on location because we wanted to take advantage of the spectacular panoramic view outside the large windows. *On Her Majesty's Secret Service* is a good example of realism in the Bond series. SYD CAIN

Diamonds Are Forever is set in Las Vegas. Early on, when we were deciding what to film on location and what to build back at Pinewood, I nearly had Ken Adam in tears because we wanted to use a really tacky looking suite for a scene between Bond and Tiffany Case. Ken was worried that people would think he was responsible for the design of it. In the end, we could not shoot the scene on location and Ken got to build it to his own taste on stage. **But the city of Vegas opened up to us, partly because Cubby knew Howard Hughes.** Guy Hamilton

At that time, I was not thrilled with the architecture in Vegas. So I chose the most modern building I could find there, then increased it twice in height with a matte painting, working very closely with a great and legendary matte artist named Albert Whitlock. Ken Adam

For a long time, all I had in the script of *Live And Let Die* was, 'And then follows the most amazing boat chase you ever saw.' We were about ten days from shooting when United Artists asked, can you write that 'most amazing boat chase you ever saw'. So Guy sent me to my room to finally write the scene into the script. I remember I also had a fairly weak thing going on the script; Jamaica, where part of the story takes place, is known for coffee and I had a sequence with Bond trapped in a giant coffee grinder. I got a call from Guy Hamilton who told me about the crocodile farm and Ross Kananga... We not only used his farm but we named our villain after him. TOM MANKIEWICZ

By the time I got on to *Live And Let Die* and then *The Man With The Golden Gun*, we were struggling with where to take Bond. *For Live And Let Die*, Tom Mankiewicz, knowing that I was a jazz fiend, suggested New Orleans. And within ten minutes we came up with the jazz funeral sequence. We then trotted to Harry and Cubby's office and told them about our idea. But in order to justify the expense of filming in New Orleans, I said to Tom, what else is there apart from jazz? And he told me about the bayou and the canals and said, we could do a motorboat chase there. And I liked that idea very much because boat chases at sea or on a lake are usually difficult because you don't have any point of reference. But working a chase through the canals down in Louisiana gave you geography. So Tom wrote that into the script. By then, we had enough to justify a Bondian visit to New Orleans. GUY HAMILTON

We were scouting locations for *Live And Let Die* and we were practically on our way back to the airport when we saw a sign on the road that said: 'Trespassers will be eaten'. And we thought, that's interesting. We stopped and went in. No sooner had we gone through the gate than a big crocodile ran across my path – and I heard a voice saying, 'Stay where you are,' and it was Ross Kananga, the owner of the place. He said, 'Didn't you see the sign outside? Don't ever do that again, I've got 1,500 crocodiles on this farm!' On the farm, there was a pond. We built the island in the middle, the bridge and the laboratory. It took Ross three weeks to clear the area and to put the crocodiles in another part of the farm. We were left with a few and Ross doubled for Roger Moore when he had to run over the crocodiles. Ross never wore shoes, so we had to have a special pair made for him with non-slip soles – and he did the stunt several times because he kept slipping. At one point, a crocodile got him by the foot; he slipped out of the shoe and luckily got away. You see, crocodiles are quite intelligent and by the second take, they were waiting for him. We tried one more take and got it right. But that entire sequence and the look of it came about because of something we saw while location scouting. SYD CAIN

I had been hired to design the sets for *The Man With The Golden Gun*; I was on the underground and saw a poster with a picture of Phuket. I did not know where it was but I loved that tall pillar of stone in the middle of the water and I told Cubby about it. He thought it looked great and off we went to check it out. And that linked to an idea that I had to make the villain's den within a rock. The rock itself was built as a miniature in the tank at Pinewood studios. The top opened and out came the reflectors. So that location was a great start. We filmed the beach sequences on location. We then found a crevasse and built some steps. Once you turned the corner, you were at Pinewood Studios. That was the link. You always look for a link between the real locations and the sets. Because we were in Hong Kong, every morning, we would take the ferry and see the poor hulk of the *Queen Mary* lying on its side at 45 degrees, and Cubby came up with the idea of using it for M's office. We all thought, brilliant, let's go inside and see what we can find. We went on board but that only helped us to see that the angle is about 45 degrees. The idea was then written into the screenplay and back at Pinewood studios, I designed the sets, corridors and M's office, and built them at a 45-degree angle. But it was really being on location and seeing the *Queen Mary* every day that gave us the idea of using it as M's office. All the waterways you see in the boat chase in the film are there on the edge of Bangkok. And you have to equate whether it's cheaper to build it into a studio or to use the actual location. In this case, we kept it down to a certain number of crossings, and therefore, we were able to control the location. The locals were very cooperative. And it was the right thing to do. Building it on a studio lot would have been a monumental task. PETER MURTON

Int. M's Cabin - Q.E.I.

For Your Eyes Only was my first Bond as director. As a rule, the first thing I did when I went on a location scout was to go to a local store and look at the postcards. And that's how I selected all those special places in the film. For *The Living Daylights,* we went to Morocco to do the Afghanistan-set Russian base-camp sequences, and we were very lucky because we had a storm there and after three days, the wind died down and the mountains surrounding us were all covered with snow, which looked exactly like Afghanistan. One of the key action scenes was done using a foreground miniature bridge. It was built at Pinewood and brought over to Morocco on a truck. We spent about two weeks setting it all up. And we gave the impression that the bridge was about three hundred feet high. That's an old-fashioned technique. Peter Lamont and his brother Michael were in charge of the foreground miniature. We also worked with John Richardson in the special effects department, and we had the planes and explosions going off... I always felt this was the ultimate in foreground miniature. John Glen

Michael Wilson always has locations and action sequences in mind. For instance, on *GoldenEye*, he mentioned the dish which is on the island of Puerto Rico, near Arecibo. It is the world's largest spherical radio telescope. And I suggested staging the ending of the film there, where you have the villain Trevelyan hanging from the antenna. Martin Campbell

One of the reasons why I love to be a designer is that you get to scout locations. On *Tomorrow Never Dies*, we went to North Vietnam, South Vietnam, Indonesia and so on. Ultimately, we were not allowed to film in Vietnam and decided to go to Thailand, because we had done *Air America* there and within three weeks we had new locations. We shot some of the interiors of Carver's headquarters, like the party at the beginning of the film, in a real location. We must have looked at forty or fifty different places before we found the one you see in the film. When I saw the different levels, the slick transparent look of it, I instinctively knew this was the place. In many cases, you don't overanalyze things, you just go with your gut reaction. ALLAN CAMERON

On *Die Another Day*, we shot scenes in Cadiz, Spain – standing in for Havana. We tried to be faithful and true to what Havana is really like and the biggest compliment I received was when a colleague called, asking how we had got on in Havana. When I said that we had shot it in Spain, they just couldn't believe it! *Casino Royale* was filmed for several weeks on location in the Bahamas, including at the One and Only Club where Bond plays poker with the villain Dimitrios and wins his Aston Martin. The Bahamas also doubles for Madagascar, where we staged an amazing action sequence. It was particularly interesting for me to go back to the Bahamas since I had worked on *Thunderball* and *The Spy Who Loved Me* and both were partly filmed there. Other locations on the film include Venice and Lake Como in Italy. We also recreated a Miami airfield in Dunsford, England and in Prague. PETER LAMONT

One of the most memorable gadgets in the Bond series was Little Nellie in *You Only Live Twice*. It was brought to us by Wing Commander Wallis – he invented it and flew it for us in the film. It was not created for the film; it already existed and was incorporated into the script after we saw a demonstration of it. But it was very difficult to film because it depended on the winds and we also had the sun to contend with. So we used about four or five cameras on it flying for real and later on, we did the close-ups with Sean on a soundstage. LEWIS GILBERT

210 Auto giro approaching mainland.

211 Autogiro over Volcanoes

212 Cockpit – Bond – 'Nothing here except Vulcanoes'

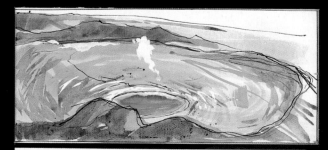

213 Bonds P.o.v. of THE Vulcano.

213 a) Circles rim of Volcano.

213 b) Starts to climb.

On *From Russia With Love*, we had rudimentary gadgets: for Bond's attaché case where he hides the knife, and the sovereign coins, I just took a regular suitcase and cannibalized it for the film. Lotte Lenya's famous lethal shoe was also very simple. I just added a spike to the right shoe and built in a spring mechanism that popped it out. SYD CAIN

Michael Wilson is a science nut and fastidious about engineering inventions.
A lot of the great things that have been invented in the films have come out of his fertile imagination. And he can find a scientific reason behind any gadget.
For him, the gadget has to have foundation in physics or engineering.

It can't just exist for its own sake.

LEE TAMAHORI

A CHRISTMAS PRESENT
FROM JAMES BOND

A solid gold fountain pen that screws into the body of a gold cigarette lighter. A gold cigarette case that is snapped into place to form a handle. A solid gold cuff link that becomes the trigger. A single gold bullet that is placed in the chamber.

THE BARREL OF THE GUN. A SOLID GOLD FOUNTAIN PEN

THE HAMMER AND BULLET CHAMBER.
A SOLID GOLD CIGARETTE LIGHTER

THE
MAGAZINE
HAND GRIP
A SOLID GOLD
CIGARETTE
CASE

THE MAN
WITH THE
GOLDEN GUN
IS READY TO
ASSASSINATE
JAMES BOND

THE TRIGGER
A SOLID GOLD CUFF LINK

HARRY SALTZMAN and ALBERT R. BROCCOLI present
ROGER MOORE as
JAMES BOND
IAN FLEMING'S
007 "THE MAN
WITH THE
GOLDEN GUN"
Directed by GUY HAMILTON
United Artists

FOR CHRISTMAS—1974

Scaramanga's gun in *The Man With The Golden Gun* was a great gadget and the design of it evolved over time. We said, he carries a pen, a lighter, etc… and we put them all on the table and we realized that the objects added up to something that looked like a gun. The pen could be a gun barrel, the lighter could be the handle, and so on. So we went to a jewellery maker who came up with a way to fit them all together. It sounds simple but it took a long time. And once we had a prototype that we were all happy with, we had to make several guns; one that fired blanks, one to rehearse with, etc… For Bond's Walther PPK, we used real ones that were doctored to fire blanks. PETER MURTON

For the Q sequence in *Die Another Day*, it was my idea to have the retro piece with the room full of the old gadgets. I wanted to have humour at the expense of previous Bonds. Most of the gadgets you see are real, including Rosa Klebb's shoe. If you look at it, it's just a simple little contraption for the spike to come out but all of us on the set were looking at it in awe and wonderment. It was for the fans but also an opportunity to inject some humour. We loved the idea of having Bond lovingly going through the objects but we did not want him to say things like, I remember this and I remember that. It had to be oblique, or something like, 'Does this thing still work?' when touching the jetpack from *Thunderball*. LEE TAMAHORI

There aren't many gadgets in *Casino Royale*, and no Q. But we have the Medipac – which, in the film, is a device that allows MI6 to monitor Bond's condition after he's been poisoned, while he is still in the field. And it's a real thing; the people who invented it are actually members of the Broccoli family and it was irresistible, it was something we had to use in the story. ROBERT WADE

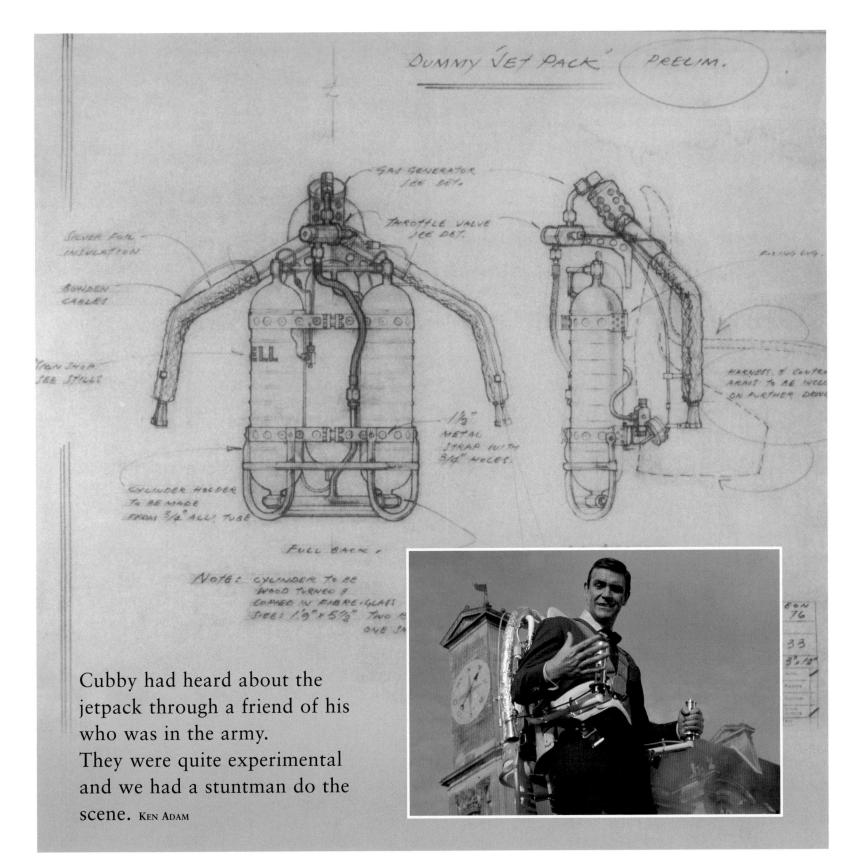

DUMMY 'JET PACK'   PRELIM.

GAS GENERATOR
ICE DET.

THROTTLE VALVE
ICE DET.

SILVER FOIL
INSULATION

BOWDEN
CABLES

FIXING LUG.

...TION SHOP.
SEE STILLS

HARNESS & CONTRO...
ARMS TO BE INCL...
ON FURTHER DRW...

1½"
METAL
STRAP WITH
¾" HOLES.

CYLINDER HOLDER
TO BE MADE
FROM ¾" ALU. TUBE

FULL BACK.

NOTE: CYLINDER TO BE
WOOD TURNED &
COPIED IN FIBREGLASS
SIZES 1.9" X 5½" TWO R...
ONE S...

Cubby had heard about the
jetpack through a friend of his
who was in the army.
They were quite experimental
and we had a stuntman do the
scene. KEN ADAM

The car was in the script for *Goldfinger* but it only had smoke coming out of the back during the chase. We all thought that we really could load up this car with gadgets. And my contribution was the revolving licence plate. I was getting a lot of parking tickets, and I absolutely dreamed of getting a ticket and, as I drove away, the licence plate would revolve in the face of the meter maid.

Everybody chipped in with their ideas for gadgets – even my stepson, who mentioned he had seen an ejector seat on TV. Guy Hamilton

My theory was, don't tell the audience what the car can do, just cut away to Sean's boredom and let's surprise the audience with the gadgets later. But Cubby did not agree – he thought we should tell the audience what the car could do and so we wrote additional dialogue for Q, lines like, 'No matter what, don't touch that red switch,' and so on. And of course, Cubby was absolutely right: tell them what you're going to do and then do it. Guy Hamilton

With Bond, it was always a question of finding things that are normally used and making them Bondian, which usually meant turning them around the opposite way. For instance, Q gives to Bond all kinds of props with a very specific purpose in mind, but then of course Bond uses them in some illogical way. A perfect example is the Aston Martin in *Goldfinger*. Before that, gadgets were not really part of Bond's world.

Guy Hamilton

Bond Worlds: the cars

I had a great effects man named John Stears. John was an engineer. For the Aston Martin, I did a sketch, and Johnny basically made it work. With each film, the special effects department became more and more important. I remember we initially discussed what kind of car we should give Bond. We considered the Bentley which was in the Fleming novels. But then we decided it would be nice if he had the latest sports car and since this was a British production, rather than using a Ferrari or a Maserati, we decided on the Aston Martin. Johnny Stears and I went to Aston Martin to get two cars, one for the driving, one for the special effects. We encountered some resistance at first, but then Cubby and Harry talked to them and they did finally agree to let us use the car. And of course, after the film came out, their sales went up. With the car in *Goldfinger*, gadgets became an integral part of the Bond films. KEN ADAM

My favourite Bond film is *Goldfinger*. I own a DB9 Aston Martin and the only reason why I have it is because of James Bond. STEVEN SPIELBERG

Scaramanga's car transforming into an airplane in *The Man With The Golden Gun* was achieved in the editing room. The cuts give the illusion of the transformation. The car drives into the hangar, then just as the police arrive, out of the doors comes the plane. We built the wings on the actual car, a stuntman drove it out to the runway and then we cut to a radio-controlled model built by John Stears, which was about 7 to 8 feet wide, and off it went. PETER MURTON

After *Moonraker* and my years as an art director on Bond, I graduated to production designer on *For Your Eyes Only* and Cubby's edict to me was going back to basics. That's why we used a Citroën 'Deux Cheveaux' for the big car chase, as opposed to a car loaded with gadgets. PETER LAMONT

On *GoldenEye*, I felt we had to bring back the Aston Martin DB5. For me, the car spelled out: we know who we are. I got to drive it with Samantha Bond. It smelled of oil and leather. It was exactly the way you imagined it would be. BRUCE FEIRSTEIN

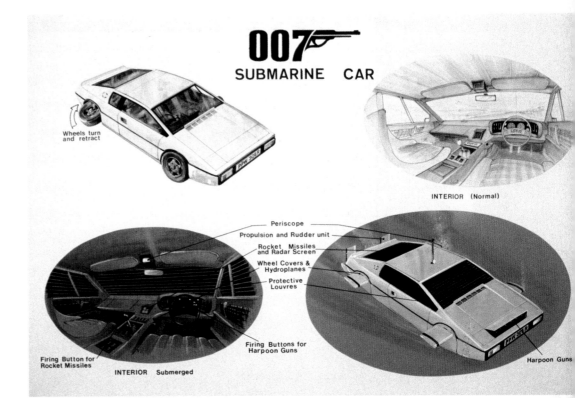

007

SUBMARINE CAR

Wheels turn and retract

INTERIOR (Normal)

Periscope
Propulsion and Rudder unit
Rocket Missiles and Radar Screen
Wheel Covers & Hydroplanes
Protective Louvres

Firing Button for Rocket Missiles

INTERIOR Submerged

Firing Buttons for Harpoon Guns

Harpoon Guns

When I was working on *The Spy Who Loved Me*, I owned a Lotus car – an older model – and a new one called the Esprit had just come out. I thought, apart from it being a fabulous sports car, that its shape could make it believable as a submarine. I started sketching and an American submarine company built it for me. And it travelled underwater – it was not pressurized but it could do seven knots underwater. Stunt drivers with oxygen tanks operated it and we also had it as a model. The interior shots with the actors were shot on a soundstage. KEN ADAM

On *Tomorrow Never Dies*, there was a chase sequence inside a parking lot involving Bond and his new BMW 75OiL. I was on my way to location with the director, Roger Spottiswoode and I suddenly came up with the idea of a chase through the different levels of the parking garage with the car ending up on the roof, flying off and crashing into the other side of the street. And all of this with Bond driving the car with a remote control. For each of the levels in the parking structure, I dreamed up something different. And it took thirty-five minutes, the length of our ride to the location, to come up with all this. Once we arrived, I told Barbara how I had thought of this chase through seven levels of the parking structure. She was puzzled at first but I told her not to worry. What we ended up doing is, instead of filming on different levels – which would have cost a fortune and taken a month to do – we stayed on one level and kept on making it look different. Of course, the car was not really worked by remote control but that's what we wanted the audience to believe. We hid lipstick cameras on the outside of the vehicle that transmitted the image to a stuntman who was lying flat inside the car and driving it by watching several monitors. The worst part of it was that the stuntman got motion sickness after a while! Another aspect of that sequence was the camera vehicle that had to be created in order to capture the action. Old camera cars – insert cars as we call them – are archaic. They're very heavy, not fast enough. So I asked Dave Bickers, a fantastic guy who has a huge business rigging vehicles for films, to build me an insert car with enough room for the director, a driver and the camera crew that could move very fast. And so he built us this sports car with hard suspension and it worked beautifully. VIC ARMSTRONG

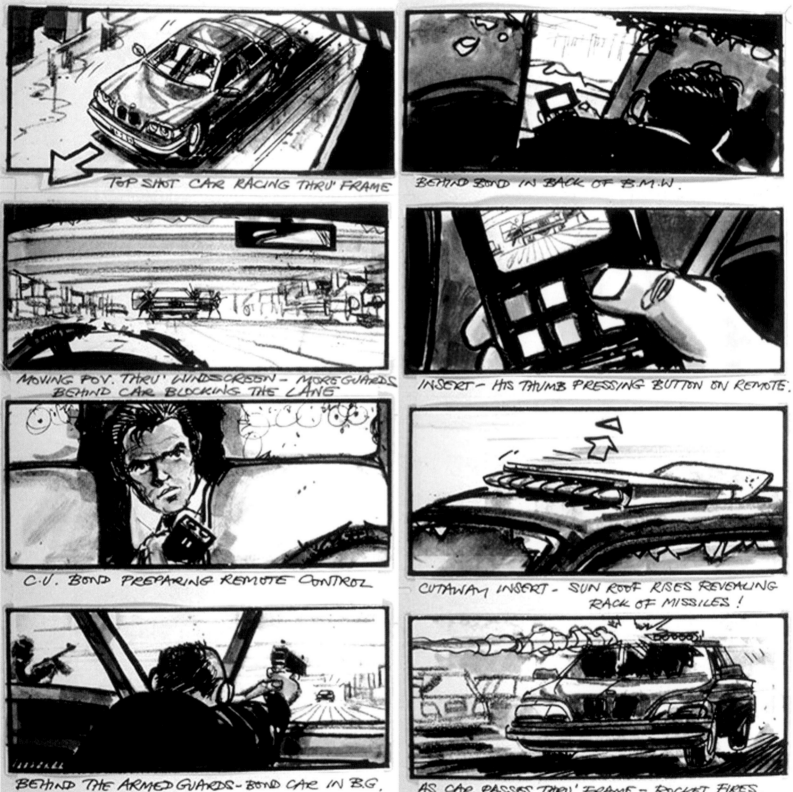

TOP SHOT CAR RACING THRU' FRAME

BEHIND BOND IN BACK OF B.M.W.

MOVING P.O.V. THRU' WINDSCREEN - MORE GUARDS
BEHIND CAR BLOCKING THE LANE

INSERT - HIS THUMB PRESSING BUTTON ON REMOTE.

C.U. BOND PREPARING REMOTE CONTROL

CUTAWAY INSERT - SUN ROOF RISES REVEALING
RACK OF MISSILES !

BEHIND THE ARMED GUARDS - BOND CAR IN B.G.

AS CAR PASSES THRU' FRAME - ROCKET FIRES.

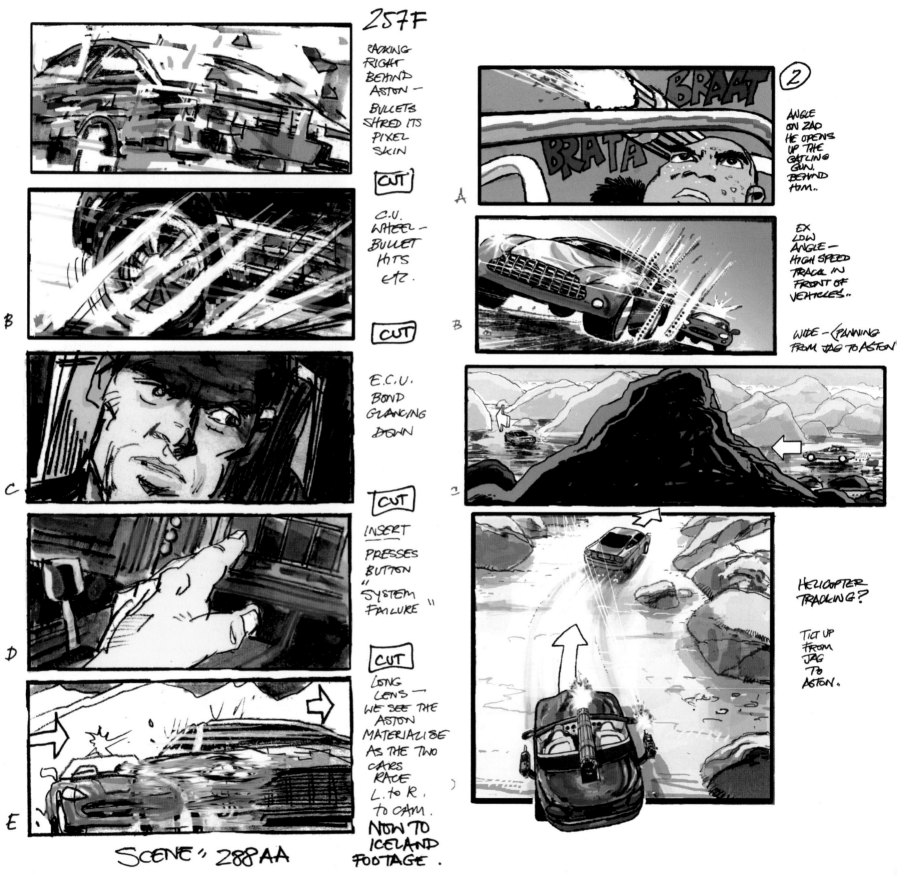

257F

RACKING RIGHT BEHIND ASTON —
BULLETS SHRED ITS PIXEL SKIN

CUT

C.U. WHEEL — BULLET HITS ETC.

CUT

E.C.U. BOND GLANCING DOWN

CUT

INSERT PRESSES BUTTON "SYSTEM FAILURE"

CUT

LONG LENS — WE SEE THE ASTON MATERIALIZE AS THE TWO CARS RACE L. TO R. TO CAM. NOW TO ICELAND FOOTAGE.

SCENE: 288 AA

②

ANGLE ON ZAO HE OPENS UP THE GATLING GUN BEHIND HIM..

EX LOW ANGLE — HIGH SPEED TRACK IN FRONT OF VEHICLES..

WIDE — (PANNING FROM JAG TO ASTON

HELICOPTER TRACKING?

TILT UP FROM JAG TO ASTON.

The car is a big component of the James Bond brand. Everyone wants to know, what is James Bond's next car going to be? For *Die Another Day*, given that it was our 40th Anniversary year, we did make a conscious effort to return to our roots with the Aston Martin heritage. KEITH SNELGROVE

In designing the car-chase scene in *Die Another Day*, I thought, I've got two beautiful cars. They have the same technology so they can't outplay each other – so the chase has to be like a chess game. Then I looked at the location and the beautiful icebergs and I devised this sort of ballet on ice between the two cars. I did a diagram, as I always do, and looked for highs and lows, the build-up and the climax. Each action sequence has to have a structure – just like a story. VIC ARMSTRONG

Ford was doing the cars – and they own Jaguar, Volvo, Aston Martin, Range Rover… It's a huge list so you have a lot to draw from. We decided to go for the Aston Martin. We also had an XKR Jaguar and our initial idea was much more futuristic and we had to scale it back a little. The Aston Martin was born in *Goldfinger* and we kept trying to come up with new gadgets for it. LEE TAMAHORI

There is a battlefield invention called 'adoptive camouflage'. On the side of a tank, you've got an array of sensors and they photograph what's on one side, and project the image back onto itself. So suddenly, the tank is almost invisible and we simply transposed the concept to the car that Bond drives. PETER LAMONT

Bond's origins. For instance, in the past few films, we've had him drive an Aston Martin DB5 as his personal car, so in this story we reveal how he acquired it. MICHAEL G. WILSON

Making It Real: the team, the actors, filming the action

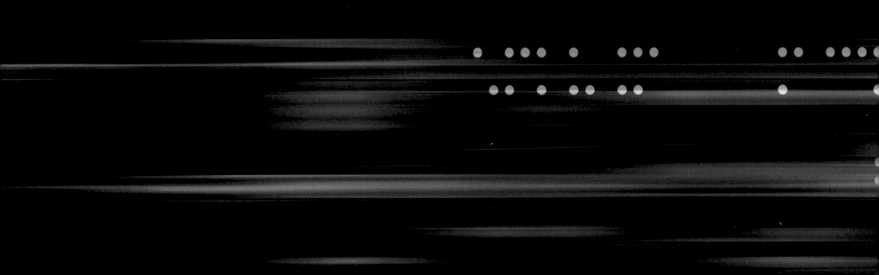

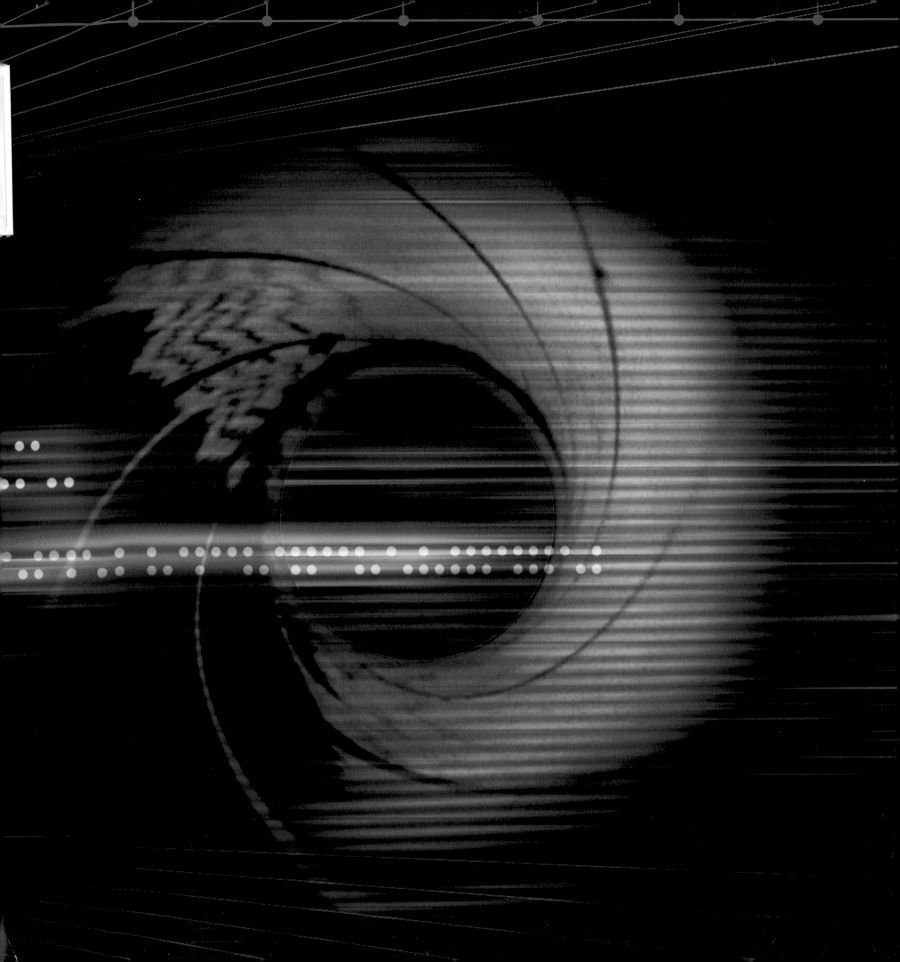

Cubby chose crew from previous films he had made. He knew who was reliable and who could give him what he needed. The teams were put together very thoughtfully. They were people he respected.

He would see the potential in people and would always stand by them. MICHAEL G. WILSON

Cubby was always very popular with the crew. The great secret was that people respected Cubby. He was very clever and could get the best out of people and he certainly got the best out of me. I first met Cubby when I was filming second unit photography for the bobsleigh sequence in Switzerland for *On Her Majesty's Secret Service*. Cubby had gone to check how the other unit was doing; they were filming the ski sequence and it was very repetitive. Cubby took a helicopter and came to see how we were doing on the bob run and he found that much more to his liking. And he liked it so much, he asked to take a ride in the bobsleigh; I couldn't believe it.

But he did it and he loved it. JOHN GLEN

Making It Real: the team

Harry Saltzman and Cubby Broccoli produced the early Bonds together and they were a great double act. Harry was a great circus man and believed in the show. His motto was, 'Bring on the elephants' and he meant it quite literally. GUY HAMILTON

The first Bond film I ever saw was *Dr No*, on a re-release. My parents didn't really take me to the movies when I was growing up. And we lived in a very small town in New Zealand with no movie theatre. In those days, we never had Bond films shown on television either. We were very isolated but then, around 1970, *Dr No* was re-released as a double feature with *The Dam Busters*. After I saw the film, I immediately started reading the books and became a big fan of Bond through the novels. I remember being very impressed with the novels of *Moonraker, Thunderball* and *On Her Majesty's Secret Service*. In 1973, I saw *Live and Let Die* when it was first released. I was about twelve years old and I thought the film was very exciting and terrific. I kept reading the novels and got a book called *James Bond in the Cinema* by John Brosnan. I read all about the other Bond movies I had never seen and since I had no access to them, I imagined them by looking at photographs and posters. *The Man With The Golden Gun* came out and I saw it four times in a row, and around that time, I joined the cinema club when I went to high school. And one of the things we could do was choose 16mm prints that were available to rent from a catalogue and every month we would select a film to show the other students to raise money. I found to my amazement that they had 16mm prints of the old Bond films. At that stage, I had my own 16mm projector so when we rented a print of *From Russia With Love* for the school, I asked the teacher if I could borrow it. That weekend, I ran it about six times on a white sheet on the wall of my bedroom. Then, around 1975, there was a major re-release of all of the old Bond films at a cinema nearby. I just went and watched each of them two or three times and caught up with all the ones I had missed up to that date. I was the perfect age to experience the films and in many respects, *On Her Majesty's Secret Service* was my favourite one.

And from that point forward, I watched every single new Bond film on opening day or as soon as I could. PETER JACKSON

I was a serious art student and went to Rowe College Of Art. There was a set-design class that I took as extra-curricular activity. And everyone wanted to see a big set designed by Ken Adam for *Dr No*, so we all went out to Pinewood. The first thing I saw was Sean Connery, dressed in his tuxedo, just standing there waiting and smoking a cigarette, while they were fiddling with the camera. Terence Young, the director, was dressed in a navy blue, very smart blazer with gold buttons, polished shoes, a button-down shirt, a tie, hair plastered down and he was shouting at the top of his voice to get the whole thing moving. And it all looked so extraordinarily difficult. And that

I tried twice to get Cubby Broccoli to hire me to direct a Bond film. The first time, I met him in person after I'd done *Duel*. I told him I wanted to do a Bond picture more than anything else in the world, and he said: 'We only hire British, experienced directors!' And I failed in both categories; I was neither

It was wonderful to have a producer like Cubby who knew so much about the subject. It's a rare thing. And you could go to him and say, how about we do this and that, and he'd immediately know if it had already been done in one of the previous films. He was always around and available. He was a film-maker and a lovely man. My favourite story, which sums him up, was when we were on *The Spy Who Loved Me* in Egypt. Cubby had suggested that we get food for the crew from England. But for some mysterious reason, it never arrived, and it was a disaster. So we started shooting and I kept worrying about what would happen at lunchtime. Well, at one o'clock, we all went to the tents for lunch and saw Cubby in a chef's hat cooking spaghetti for everyone. It was a masterstroke and from then on, the crew would have done anything for him. LEWIS GILBERT

Cubby and his wife Dana were incredibly kind people. There was nothing in their house that told you that Cubby was Bond except for the Thalberg Award. But when you asked Cubby a question about Bond, he was always delighted to talk about it. You could even be honest about things you did not like. He loved the fact that the films, even years later, evoked passion in people. Cubby was incredibly generous. Dana was also very smart; she would come into my office and just say, 'Write funnier.' They lived a big life and I have enormous respect for both of them. BRUCE FEIRSTEIN

Tomorrow Never Dies is dedicated to Cubby; unfortunately, he passed away before I got started so I never got to meet him. But certainly working with Barbara and Michael, I immediately felt the family spirit and atmosphere. Until then, I was used to producers being in the background, but Barbara and Michael were involved in every aspect of the film. They're very supportive. ALLAN CAMERON

Barbara and Michael have managed to continue Cubby's legacy. What's great about them as producers is that they don't have a personal agenda; or their only agenda is to keep the franchise going. And I immediately learned to trust them. They're the ones who kept Bond on track; I'd say to them, why doesn't Bond do this? And they would explain why Bond would not do that, and you have to trust the huge knowledge that they bring to it. MICHAEL APTED

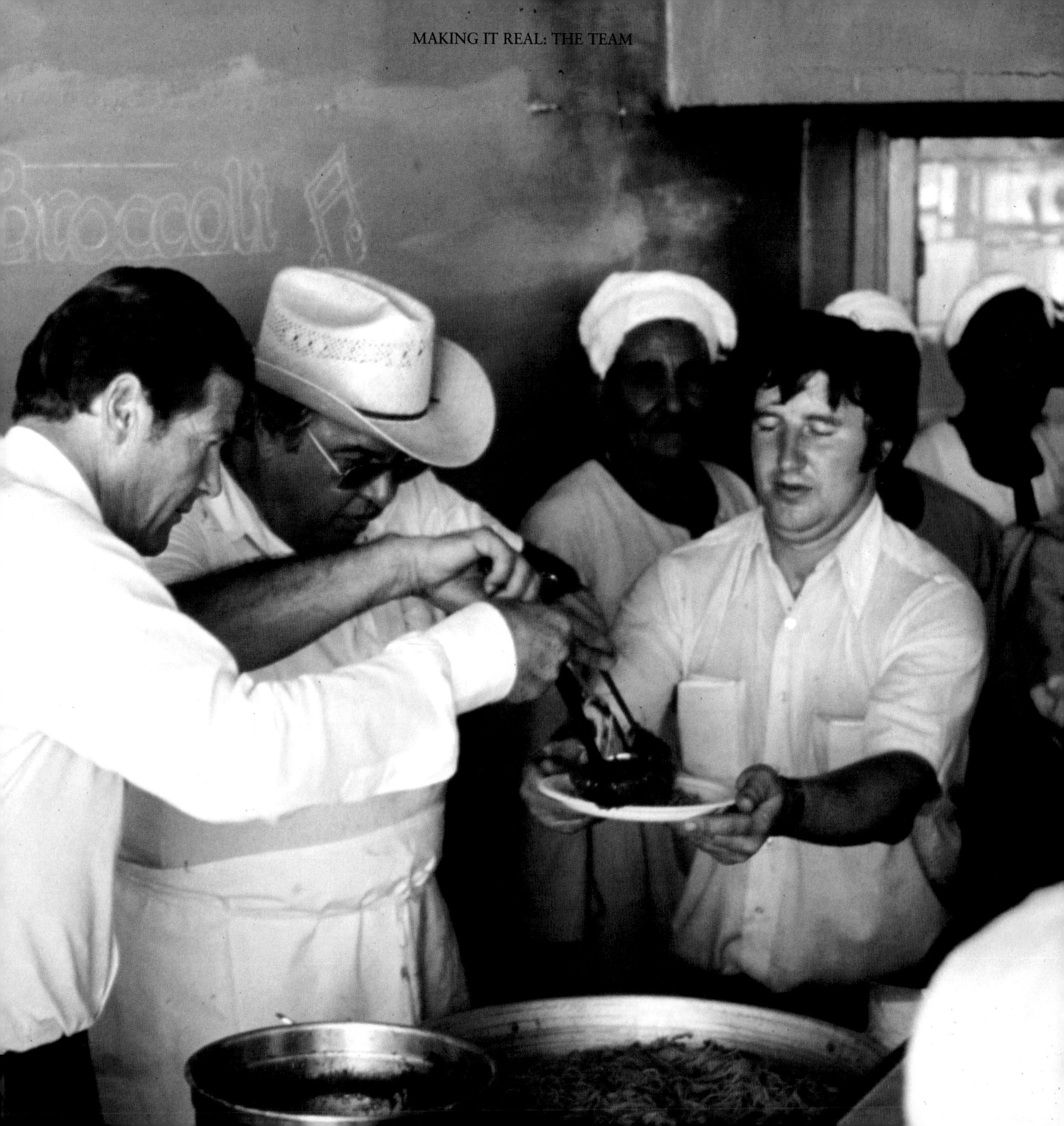
Broccoli

When you're making a movie, every person in every job reads the script. If you're the production designer, you try to imagine how you're going to tell the story and how you're going to introduce the characters. A prop guy wants to make sure that the cigarette lighter reflects Bond's character, the costume designer wants to make sure that all the things that Bond is wearing will reflect his personality. Everybody comes to it from their point of view and wanting to tell their story, which is why the films are so complicated to make and why people take such pride in their own personal contribution. It's a very collaborative effort. Because we're a series, we set certain parameters. We feel that the audience has expectations that we need to fulfil and we need someone who will come along and have his own distinctive style but can work within the expectations and still have a stamp of creativity on the film. We try to find directors who are good storytellers because the plots are so complex. We need someone with a vision and someone who can explain the vision, someone who can lead a group around the world, someone who can manage many units shooting at the same time, someone who is good with actors and humour. BARBARA BROCCOLI

My involvement with *Goldfinger* was fairly simple. I had known Cubby and Harry for some time. Cubby had offered me *Dr No* and sent me the script. I thought it was great fun but the story involved filming on location in Jamaica and at that time, I had personal problems and I could not leave the UK. I saw the picture and enjoyed it. But I felt that *From Russia With Love* was terrific and better; they had realized that there was a humorous side to Bond and that you could not play it straight. And then, they called me again to see if I would be interested in *Goldfinger* – and I was. I also had great people working with me; among them Ted Moore, who was a wonderful director of photography. I had met him when I was an assistant director on films like *The African Queen*. He was a pleasure to work with. We both understood that Bond had to be glossy. GUY HAMILTON

Terence Young directed the first Bond film. Everyone, including Cubby, always gave credit to Terence Young's vision, he was someone who had an element of class and culture, someone who knew how to work with Sean Connery and bring out the establishing traits of the James Bond character. The world described in the early Bond films was part of the world that Cubby, Harry and Terence inhabited. Michael G. Wilson

When Cubby started making *Dr No*, he had very little money. They had to move fast and they had to be quite efficient. There was no time to hang around. They knew they had to do something to make it exciting and one of the ways was through editing. Peter Hunt – who edited many of the Bond films, including *Dr No*, and directed *On Her Majesty's Secret Service* – brought in a style of cutting that shocked people. Sean Connery would look towards a door and then you'd cut and he'd be outside the door, walking down a corridor. It was an abbreviated type of film-making. So Peter Hunt was part of the original team that started it all, along with Cubby and Harry, Terence Young, Ken Adam, John Barry with the music and Maurice Binder, who designed the titles. JOHN GLEN

I'd made several big pictures, and I had just made *Alfie* when Cubby and Harry came to me and asked me to do Bond number five. At first, I turned them down because I did not know what I could possibly offer them. Cubby called and told me he was surprised at my reaction, because, he said, he was interested in seeing what sort of mess I'd make of it. And that immediately appealed to me. He said, 'You're turning down the biggest audience in the world.' And I thought, that's absolutely true. When you make a film, you never know what the audience is going to be. You might make a good picture and nobody goes to see it. You may make a bad one and everybody goes to see it. There's no science to it. But what Cubby did say was that there was a big audience worldwide waiting to see the next Bond film. And so I accepted the offer and it became a huge success. In the case of *You Only Live Twice*, we were filming in very exotic locations in Japan and I thought we could take the photography a step further, and so to have Freddie Young as our director of photography, whom I knew quite well, was a logical choice. He was very keen to participate because he had never done anything like this before – he loved the idea of doing a real thriller with beautiful photography. I had Claude Renoir, a French director of photography, on *The Spy Who Loved Me*, who was not only brilliant but also quite fast. He was going to do *Moonraker* but he had a degenerative eye disease that eventually blinded him and suggested we replace him with Jean Tournier, who was also very good. LEWIS GILBERT

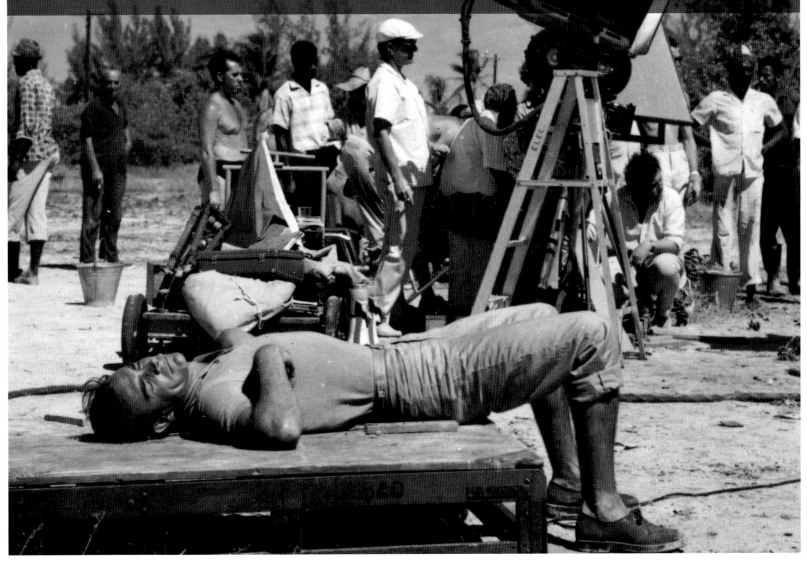

I was asked to do *GoldenEye* because Barbara Broccoli and Michael Wilson had seen a movie I did called *No Escape*. The movie did not make any money but I think they thought enough of it and of *Edge of Darkness*, a television series I did, to give me the job. I loved the books – I had read all of them early on, and I was a huge fan of the films. I took my mother to see *Dr No* and I remember everything about it, where we saw it, the city, the theatre. But at the time I was sceptical about doing *GoldenEye*. In retrospect, later on, I thought, how dare I even think about not doing this film! MARTIN CAMPBELL

The thing I love about doing costumes for Bond films is the odd little detail, the fact that Bond himself or a Bond girl has a weapon about their bodies, or that something has to transform into something else. Those are the challenges in designing costumes for Bond. And that means that all the departments have to work together. Whatever happens to the characters in the story will influence the costumes, the sets, everything. LINDY HEMMING

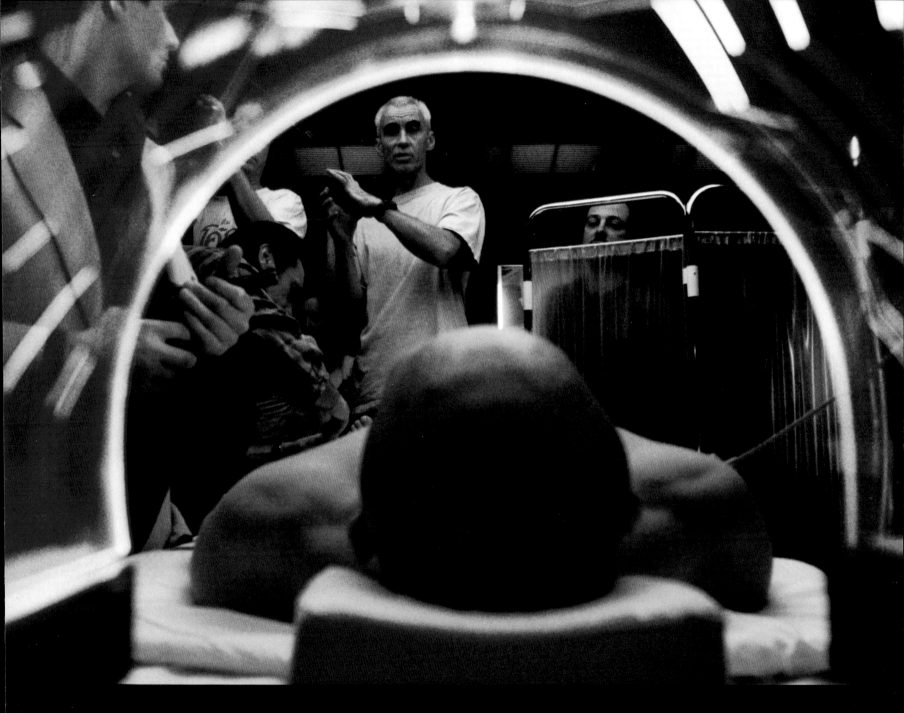

I always wanted to work with that huge pantheon of British talent. I viewed all of them as an asset. They've done it before and know the infrastructure needed to make it all happen. I grew up loving that stuff and it was a dream come true to be allowed to play with this giant train set, including the 007 stage! LEE TAMAHORI

I consider I became a man at fourteen, when Bond first came out. To me, that was the epitome of action. It had everything that I did not have: it had sophistication, foreign locations, beautiful women, fantastic cars. To me, it was my fantasy. When *Dr No* came out, I was just dreaming about being in the film business, about being a stuntman. Through my work with horses, I eventually got involved with stunts and a friend, Bill Weston said to me, why don't you go to Pinewood Studios, they're doing the new Bond film, *You Only Live Twice*. So I went and met the team: Bob Simmons, George Leech and Dicky Graydon. They explained they needed me to slide down a rope from the roof and

gave me a six-week contract. And that was my first of many experiences with Bond. I learned a lot from Bob Simmons. He was one of the few who could break down a sequence, come up with great fight scenes like the one between Connery and Robert Shaw in the train carriage in *From Russia With Love*. Working with Bob was the first time I saw anyone do 'the exchange', where a stuntman takes a fall, runs behind a barrel and out comes Sean Connery. We still use those tricks. On *You Only Live Twice*, Bob used trampolines and we still do. Stunts in those days were more innovative; we had no CGI and we did it all for real.
VIC ARMSTRONG

After *GoldenEye*, I did not want to do another Bond until Barbara and Michael approached me for *Casino Royale*. I felt it was a return to the old James Bond, something real, perhaps closer to *From Russia With Love*. MARTIN CAMPBELL

When I was brought in to direct *The World Is Not Enough*, I made sure I had all the people who had some history with Bond working with me, from the first assistant through to Peter Lamont and Vic Armstrong. All of them had a lot of history and a lot of information and I was very dependent on that. MICHAEL APTED

To audition new actors for the role of Bond, we have them do the scene in *From Russia With Love*, where he first meets Tatiana Romanova in the bedroom. It's very sexy, and tough at the same time. We also do stunt scenes, and we try to see what the actor looks like in a tuxedo and how he throws a punch. MICHAEL G. WILSON

The films have introduced many faces to the public and we have had a long tradition of discovering a new Bond, new villains, new women. And it is very exciting to comb the universe looking for the right people. We're constantly being told by actors, that ever since they were little boys, they wanted to be James Bond. We even meet regular people who are not actors who tell us they say 'Bond, James Bond' in front of the mirror when they're shaving in the morning. BARBARA BROCCOLI

I've always said that the easiest part for me was working with the actors, because their contribution was so enormous. Lewis Gilbert once said to me, 'If you ever get into a situation where you're not sure what you want to do with a scene, then get the actors to the set. The second you say 'Action!' they'll start doing something and then you can start shaping things from there.' JOHN GLEN

When I saw Connery's picture in the newspapers announcing that he was James Bond, I thought he was too handsome. I had pictured someone more rugged looking. Bond's hair in the books always fell forward on his forehead in a comma of black hair. And I thought that was a very distinctive feature and Connery did not have it. But that initial reaction did not survive the first twenty minutes of the film because the movie exercised its enchantment and bang, I was converted to the movies and Sean Connery as quickly as I had been to the books. KEN FOLLETT

Peter Hunt had been my editor on several of my films. One day, he told me he had been hired to work on the first Bond film. I got curious about who was going to play Bond and Peter told me that Sean Connery had been cast in the part. I was a bit surprised because I didn't immediately picture him as Bond; I knew Sean socially and had seen some of his work. But Sean had the advantage of Terence Young, who understood the world of Bond and who managed to dress him up and coach him appropriately. And he worked out very well. LEWIS GILBERT

When I was working on *Indiana Jones and the Last Crusade*, I wanted it to be a father-son story and I could think of no better father for Indiana Jones than James Bond. That's why we chose Sean Connery for the part. STEVEN SPIELBERG

Sean Connery was physically correct for the part and had enough class and enough working-class to make his portrayal of the character right and accessible to the audience. RIDLEY SCOTT

Sean made huge progress between each film. By the time he got to *Goldfinger*, he was both an accomplished comedian and an action man; he moved beautifully. There was very little for me to do, and my worry was always the people around him; most of the girls, for instance, had very little or no acting experience, so you had to be careful. But Sean and I got along very well, although I do remember one instance during the filming of *Goldfinger* where we had a bit of a situation. There was a scene where Oddjob squeezes a golf ball and reduces it to powder. Sean said it was ridiculous. And I remember explaining to him that was the whole point; I said, the audience knows that at some point you and Oddjob are going to have a head-to-head and I'm trying to say that every Bond has a problem. We went ahead with the scene and it worked brilliantly. GUY HAMILTON

I liked George Lazenby very much in *On Her Majesty's Secret Service*. I particularly remember the scene with the Saint Bernard at the end of the bobsled sequence. I did the second unit on that particular scene. We were losing the light and I knew I could only have George Lazenby for one hour, so we took a helicopter to the other side of the mountain where we had an additional hour of sunshine. George arrived; we set up the camera and I said to him, 'We'll probably have only one shot at this.' I knew from working with animals on many television series that they don't like rehearsals and they don't do many takes. So I told George to improvize and he was very good. The dog came about and started licking George's face and he simply said the line, 'Never mind that, how about the brandy?' And it worked great on take one. John Glen

Sean left Bond after *Diamonds Are Forever*, and Harry Saltzman wanted Burt Reynolds. Cubby disagreed and said, there is no reason for James Bond if he is not British. They had gone to Roger Moore twice already but he'd had other commitments. Eventually he became available. One decision we made was that he had to be different from Sean. When Sean was Bond, you could have him kiss a girl and then kill her. With Roger, the emphasis was on humour. TOM MANKIEWICZ

With Roger, I was always trying to give him a Cary Grant-like attitude. And it was the right thing to do. LEWIS GILBERT

It's a real challenge to replace an actor playing James Bond. Sean Connery was so good in the role that it was a challenge to replace him. George Lazenby was a model, top of his game, but he was not an actor. So to introduce him Peter Hunt, who directed the film, went to great lengths to make him mysterious. The audience had never seen this guy so, in the opening sequence, Peter kept cheating by just showing him lighting up a cigarette, and then suddenly he revealed him in a dramatic way. I faced a similar challenge with introducing Timothy Dalton as the new Bond in *The Living Daylights*. Tim is a huge Fleming fan and he wanted to be different from Roger Moore and Sean Connery; he wanted to be his own man. He went back to the roots of Bond and explored the character very carefully. He is a hell of a talent. JOHN GLEN

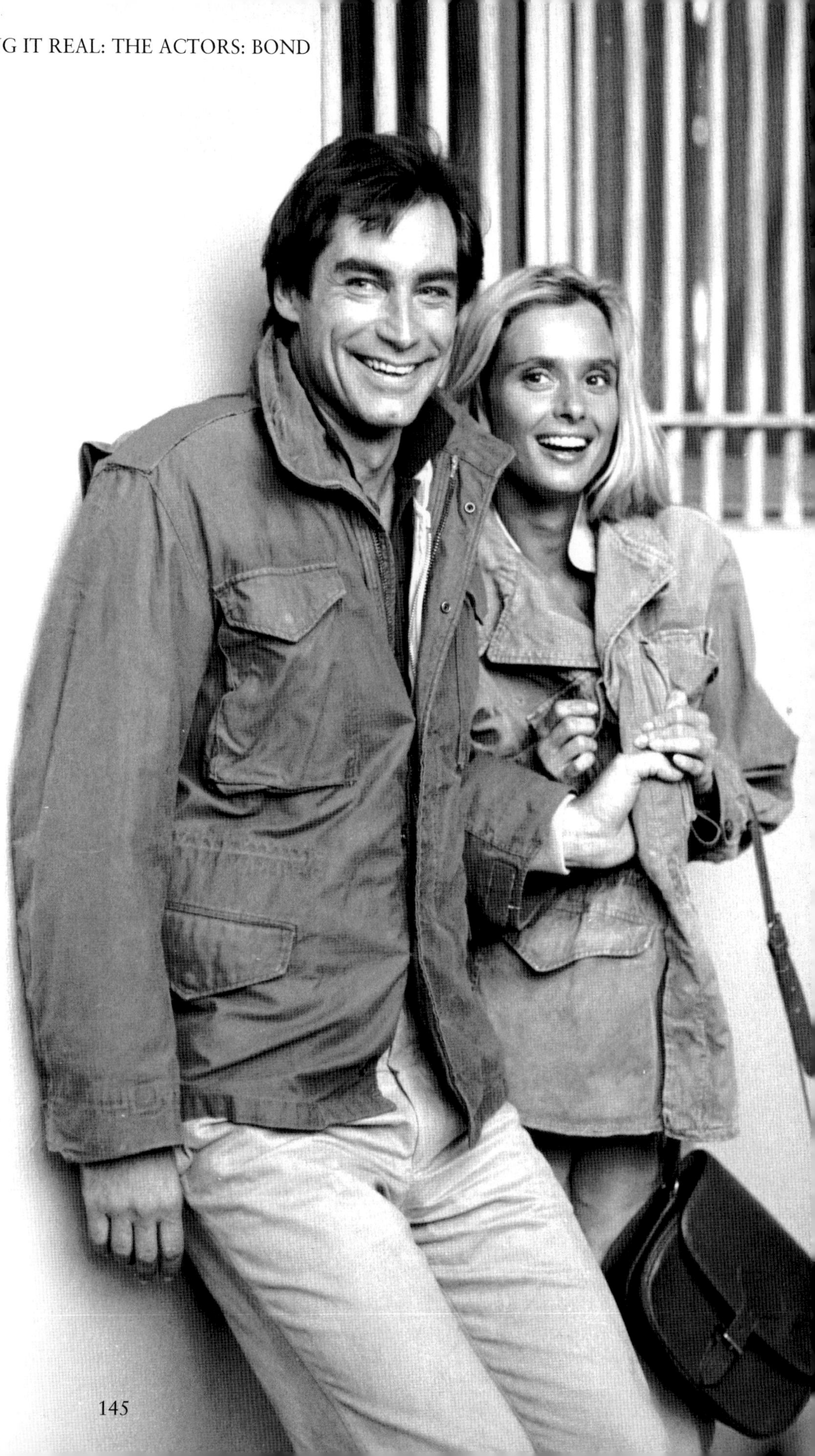

For *GoldenEye*, we chose Pierce Brosnan. I worked with Pierce the way I approach any actors; I go through the script and we discuss it. The thing about Bond is that you want him to be very comfortable in his own skin. He never fumbles, he is precise. 'Keep it simple' was the idea. Pierce could handle Bond physically, but he also has great comic timing. He has a mischievous quality in his eyes. He was very clever. MARTIN CAMPBELL

Pierce Brosnan as Bond was a great choice. He had the aristocratic air required for the part but he could also be funny, nasty, romantic, and he can move between emotions fast. And that's the key to the character. *The World Is Not Enough* was a 109-day shoot and every day something was going on in terms of action, other than just doing lines. So Pierce worked very hard. And what I love most about him is that he is very respectful and generous with other actors.

MICHAEL APTED

In general, Bond has his elegant look and his action look but in *Casino Royale*, we're given the opportunity of seeing him doing things that are down and dirty. He is a much more real person and at the beginning, a lot less elegant than usual. And as the story proceeds, he arrives in the Bahamas and he begins to emerge as the character we know. I had worked with Daniel Craig on two separate occasions, so I knew him already and I was very pleased when he was cast. Daniel has this amazing interest in fashion, clothing and style. And everything we did was slightly tipped toward a more modern look. He embraced the Brioni suit; his shirts were made by Turnbull & Asser. Everything he wears in the film was made especially for him, even his T-shirts, which were done by a company called Sunspel. We also had to choose a bathing suit for him; I brought Daniel a lot of choices and the one that he liked best and looked best in, was a slimline European-look La Perla brief suit. LINDY HEMMING

I think Daniel Craig is an outstanding choice for James Bond because as an actor, he's intense and focused and most important of all, he has a naturally dry sense of humour. He's the perfect 21st-century Bond. STEVEN SPIELBERG

Daniel Craig was very easy to work with on *Casino Royale*. He was very keen to do as many of the stunts as possible. And in this film, Bond gets hurt; normally, Bond walks away with his hair perfectly in place but here, he gets roughed up, he gets beaten up. So it was a very different experience. GARY POWELL

Daniel Craig is certainly the most rugged, tough looking Bond since Sean Connery.

PETER JACKSON

Daniel Craig was an obvious choice for *Casino Royale* because he is an actor who defines his generation. He is charismatic, he is very versatile and sexy. This part is a big challenge but he has proven to us that he is an incredible Bond. BARBARA BROCCOLI

Diana Rigg as Tracy in *On Her Majesty's Secret Service* was the strongest role for any of the Bond girls. She is a great actress and her part was very well written. She was able to make you feel terrible pathos and emotion at the end when she died. It was an incredible scene. You can't beat the first appearance of Ursula Andress in *Dr No* when she comes out of the water, but to me Diana Rigg stands out above all the others. PETER JACKSON

It was often said about Bond rather cheaply that he exploited women because he was promiscuous, but I thought he was a romantic. He really cherished women and he often risked his life to protect them. KEN FOLLETT

Fleming conceived complex characters, and certainly none of the women were ever mundane. They were all fairly avant-garde. For example, Honeychile Ryder in *Dr No* was not the girl next door. She used a black widow spider to poison the man who had been abusing her... In the films, they evolved with the times. And I think women in the Bond films are becoming experts in areas that were initially predominantly only for men. BARBARA BROCCOLI

Honor Blackman is my all-time favourite Bond girl. She was tough but she wasn't a pin-up fashion model acting tough; she happened to be a beautiful woman who was a fine British actress, and the combination of beauty and talent really served that episode of Bond well. In fact, I wouldn't even call her a Bond girl; she is a classy Bond woman. Diana Rigg is my second favorite in *On Her Majesty's Secret Service* and my third is Jill St. John. I was familiar with her work on television but I fell in love with her all over again in *Diamonds Are Forever*. I thought she was great and brought a lot of humour to the role. STEVEN SPIELBERG

On *Goldfinger*, it was a pleasure working with real actresses with experience, like Honor Blackman and Shirley Eaton. Costume design was essential in defining the three different female roles in *Goldfinger*. Pussy Galore was very physical and wore trousers. Tilly Masterson was a modern young lady and was rather sporty. And Jill Masterson was painted gold! That was in the book and it became a classic image. But I remember seeing acts at the Lido, a famous music hall in Paris, where people were painted in gold or silver. It was Fleming's idea that you must leave a little spot of the skin open for aeration because otherwise you'd suffocate. It sounds wonderfully dangerous but it's nonsense. In any case, Shirley Eaton, who played Jill, showed up on the set in a bathrobe. I explained to her where I needed her to lie down, we placed pillows strategically and we were done in ten minutes. And off she went. GUY HAMILTON

Jill St. John was going to play Plenty O'Toole in *Diamonds Are Forever*. One evening, she had dinner with Guy Hamilton and he called Cubby the next day and said, 'How about Jill for Tiffany Case?' And that's how she got the part. Casting the lead Bond girl became more complicated when we came to *Live And Let Die*. I told Cubby that Diana Ross should play Solitaire and he loved the idea. But then David Picker at UA explained that there would be at least six countries in the world where we could not play the film if Bond was sleeping with a black woman. *Live And Let Die* was the introduction of Roger Moore as Bond to the audience and there was concern that the controversy would overshadow the film. So we cast Jane Seymour, but one of the supporting roles, Rosie Carver – who was originally white – became black. The story was about black people and we could not pretend that Bond would not be attracted to a black woman. We compromised a bit; they kissed and they obviously made love but you don't see them in bed together. I love the character of Rosie and I wrote for her one of my favourite lines of dialogue: after it becomes obvious that she has betrayed Bond, she says to him, 'Oh James, you would not kill me, not after what we just did.' And he replies, 'I certainly would not have killed you before.' TOM MANKIEWICZ

I insisted on casting a black actress for Rosie. And I have to take my hat off to Cubby, Harry and United Artists because that meant we had to lose a few screens in the southern States. But they backed me up with no regret. GUY HAMILTON

What was powerful in *The Spy Who Loved Me* is the relationship between Bond and the Russian agent, Anya Amasova. And the way we approached it, was to have the audience know more than Bond; he kills the Russian guy who is after him in the ski chase at the beginning, and we know that he is Anya's boyfriend – but Bond doesn't. Anya and Bond get involved and the audience knows that at some point, there will be conflict between them. That was an unusual set-up for a Bond film. CHRISTOPHER WOOD

When we were looking for the female lead in *For Your Eyes Only*, our marketing director Jerry Juroe recommended Carole Bouquet. He had seen her in *That Obscure Object Of Desire* by Luis Buñuel. She lived in Rome and so we went there and had dinner, and I was very impressed with her. One interesting thing was that she could not swim underwater. Remember, this was before CGI, so I devised a way to shoot underwater scenes without immersing her. We changed the speed of the film and used wind machines to get her hair floating. Derek Meddings, our wonderful special effects man, added the bubbles; he marked the eyepiece of the camera to indicate where the actress's mouth was and put the bubbles on undeveloped film, one frame and one bubble at a time. And the audience never knew that Carole Bouquet never went underwater! JOHN GLEN

In Bond films, it's very difficult to find a reasonably mature woman who can also act. On *The Spy Who Loved Me*, it was particularly hard. The head of UA told me about his girlfriend Barbara Bach, who had just done a test for another film. Cubby and I watched it and we thought she'd be terrific for the role. We brought her over, tested her and we gave her the part. And she worked very hard. She did not always like it when I had her do many takes – but I remember I would

tell her, believe me, you'll thank me when you see the film at the premiere. And she did. When I started working on *Moonraker*, I was in Los Angeles airport and noticed this gorgeous girl, Lois Chiles. She had been in films like *The Way We Were*, *Coma* and had just finished *Death On The Nile*. And it turned out we were sitting next to each other on the plane; we got chatting and I mentioned her to Cubby. We tested her immediately and she got the part. LEWIS GILBERT

Pam Dickson, who was casting *GoldenEye* in the US, found Famke Janssen. The other girl, the character of Natalya Simonova, was more difficult. We were three weeks away from starting production and we were in a panic, and our casting director Debbie McWilliams said, there is only one country I have not been to and that's Sweden. She flew there that night and she called me saying, I've found your girl. And it turned out to be Izabella Scorupco, who is in fact Polish and who was absolutely perfect for the part. I liked the fact that her character stands up to Bond. And Xenia Onatopp, as played by Famke, was in the true tradition of Bond villainesses: she gets her rocks off by killing people. She loves to crush people. And Famke ate that part up. MARTIN CAMPBELL

I think I was chosen to direct *The World Is Not Enough* because I had done films like *Coal Miner's Daughter* and *Gorillas in the Mist* with strong female protagonists. In contrast to Elektra, Christmas Jones was a relatively traditional Bond girl, but even though she was still the archetypal fantasy female, we did try to make sure that she actually had things to do and was not purely there as eye candy. Elektra was more organic to the plot and turned out to be a villain. Elektra and Bond were moving the story along together. Then came the question, what does Bond do to villains? He kills them. We thought, we can't have a woman as a villain and treat her differently. But we kept wondering how the audience was going to react when Bond shoots her point-blank. I had nightmares about this, and thought we would be crucified. I previewed the film five weeks after finishing shooting it and I was astonished when the audience had no issue with the death of Elektra. To play the part I wanted a European actress, but preferably not British. I auditioned a lot of competent actresses for the role, but Sophie Marceau was my number one choice. She is such a great actress that you could believe that she could be a killer and yet, she could also be charming and seductive. MICHAEL APTED

Elektra is wealthy, she is an aristocratic woman. Then you find out that she is a villainess. And so her costumes had to keep growing because her character was slowly revealed. LINDY HEMMING

With Jinx, our Bond girl in *Die Another Day*, we thought, what would happen if Bond walked into another movie? And we applied this to Jinx. Let's have her coming from her own movie. She is someone who lives in the shadow of death, she takes her pleasure where she finds it, she has no regrets. She is very much like Bond in that respect. So, it's a meeting of equals. ROBERT WADE

I'd seen Halle Berry in *Swordfish* and I thought she'd be perfect for the role of Jinx. I thought she would be dynamic enough to run head-to-head with Bond and be his equal without upstaging him. And audiences loved her in the role. Halle was extremely solid in the part. Miranda Frost, the other Bond girl in the film, started life in the screenplay as an MI6 agent who was killed in the course of the story. Then the writers came up with the idea of making her a double agent, and I loved it. For the role, we wanted a classic British girl. We ran screen tests with six girls and decided on a newcomer, Rosamund Pike. She had that perfect Oxford accent and got a rapid education in film-making. With Madonna, we thought of her for a small part after she got on board to do the title song. I told her about the part of the dominatrix fencing instructor, and she immediately said, 'I love it and I even have the costume for it!' LEE TAMAHORI

Because *Die Another Day* marked the 40th Anniversary of the Bond series, I was mindful of having a lot of references to the previous films. The most obvious one was Halle coming out of the water, which was a direct homage to Ursula Andress's entrance in *Dr No*. In the original screenplay, Jinx was swimming in a pool by a waterfall, not in the sea. Bond was driving in Cuba, stopped at a resort, and he saw her coming out of the pool. When we cast Halle, I told the writers, let's recreate one of the most iconic images in film history. We knew it was a bit risky and tricky to ask Halle to try and replicate the moment. Halle wanted to do it justice and ultimately, we filmed it in Cadiz, Spain. My mistake was that I scouted the location in the summer and I assumed the weather was warm throughout the year. But when we arrived, it was cold and raining. It was horrific. And we only got two days of sunshine to shoot all the scenes we needed to do in that location, including Halle coming out of the water. And Halle was a real trooper. She went into training specifically for this scene. LEE TAMAHORI

Through the process of working on the film, I was leading to that specific moment. I designed the bikini and it was made by La Perla, and the dress that came with it was made to my own specifications by a dressmaker. I particularly liked the white knife-belt which was made by Whitaker Malem.

LINDY HEMMING

There are three Bond women in *Casino Royale:* Vesper, Valenka and Solange and the trick in terms of creating their costumes, aside from the fact that they were all cast at the last minute, was to try and balance the kind of women they are. That's the fun and the terror of the job because you have to make sure they don't ever end up wearing the same colour and that they have their own identity. Vesper is dark, beautiful and European. Valenka is strong, tall and cool. Solange is on the edge, what I call slightly over-the-top. I chose for her a fantastic satin coral dress by an English designer called Jenny Packham; it was made in China, flown to the Bahamas, arrived twenty-four hours before it was needed, and it had to be shortened... We had quite a Bondian experience with Solange's dress. LINDY HEMMING

For Vesper in *Casino Royale*, we needed a superb actress who was also beautiful. It took some time to find her. It's a major role for the Bond series. Her relationship wth Bond in this film defines Bond's relationships with women in the future. MICHAEL G. WILSON

Finding the right actress to play Vesper in *Casino Royale* was a challenge; she is a very complex, enigmatic and dark character in the book. Bond falls in love with her, and she falls in love with him. She's probably the most interesting Bond woman ever and we cast Eva Green, who has the mysterious quality we were after. MARTIN CAMPBELL

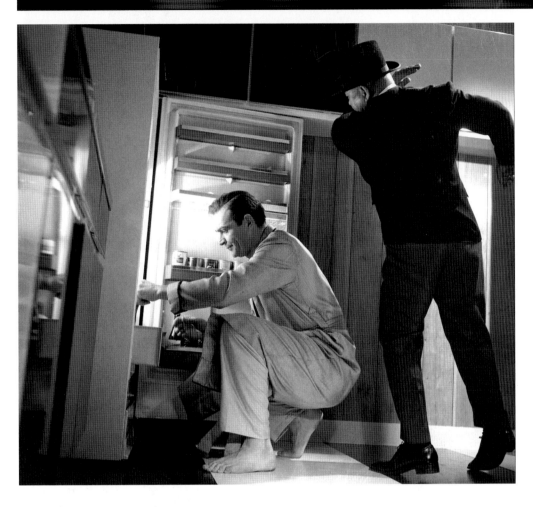

My favourite villain is Auric Goldfinger because he was a believable character. I'm also a huge fan of Donald Pleasence as Blofeld in *You Only Live Twice*. But the most potent villain was Robert Shaw in *From Russia With Love*; in a way, he is one of the most chilling villains of the Bond series, without the support of an outrageous plot device. I'm very fond of Joseph Wiseman as Doctor No; he has to be credited with creating the prototype of the Bond bad guy. His portrayal of Doctor No has largely influenced the pattern for a lot of other Bond villains that have followed in his wake. PETER JACKSON

Auric Goldfinger is my favourite villain because he wasn't afraid to show his jealousy, his envy as well as his frustration at the likes of 007. I thought he was a very vulnerable villain and if it weren't for Oddjob, he would have been defeated at the end of the first act. STEVEN SPIELBERG

We often say that the film is as good as the villain, because Bond has to have a worthy opponent and the audience has to feel that Bond is vulnerable, that the villains could possibly outwit Bond on every escapade – so it's always tough finding our next villain. BARBARA BROCCOLI

On *Goldfinger*, we had a wonderful villain in Mr Auric Goldfinger. But he was not physical. And you've got to give Bond some competition on the physical side and so we had Oddjob, who was a wonderful character. He had to be bigger and tougher than Bond. I like that Bond can have an intelligent conversation with the main bad guy, and then the villain says, 'Mr Bond, will you excuse me, I can't bear the sight of blood so I have to hand you over to my minion, who will take care of you.' And when I was casting *Goldfinger* I saw this guy, Harold Sakata, on a wrestling programme on the BBC. And Harold was the perfect match for Sean. He was an absolutely charming man, an Olympic medallist and a very proud Hawaiian. He had a very unique way of moving and in creating Oddjob I used all of Harold's own characteristics. GUY HAMILTON

...we were going mad looking for someone to play the villain, Blofeld, for *You Only Live Twice*. Anybody who was any good was already working and not available. Harry Saltzman walked in one day saying he had found the ideal man. The guy came into the office and he looked like Father Christmas. We started filming and he was terrible. Finally, an agent rang up and said, 'Donald Pleasence is available.' And he came in and was just perfect. LEWIS GILBERT

Blofeld in *Diamonds Are Forever* is very different from the way he was portrayed by Donald Pleasence in *You Only Live Twice*. Guy Hamilton selected Charles Gray, who had played a small part in *You Only Live Twice* as a totally different character who ends up with a knife in his back. I said to Charles Gray, Blofeld is like Hedda Hopper, the notorious gossip columnist. At one point we even had him dressed in drag, we had him say outrageous lines. He was sophisticated and fussy. In the film, we also had two other villains, Mr Wint and Mr Kidd. I didn't want them to be the usual thugs and I said I'd like to make these guys gay. But not in some horrible, sadistic way; they simply enjoy each other. But who could we cast? It turned out Guy Hamilton loved jazz and went to a club in Los Angeles where Putter Smith was playing the bass. He immediately saw him as Mr Kidd and offered him the part. He had never acted before and never acted again. If you were on location in Vegas and in the hotel room next to his, you'd hear him practise every day. To play his partner, we chose Bruce Glover and we had a perfect match. TOM MANKIEWICZ

In all the Bond films, at one point, the villain has to make larger-than-life statements, he or she has to be vicious and unpleasant but the villain should also be sophisticated. It is enormous fun to write that. They have to be smart, especially if your goal is to control the world. There is a fascination from the audience to see someone destroy things. It's a little bit like watching the sandcastle washed away by the sea. CHRISTOPHER WOOD

For Stromberg in *The Spy Who Loved Me*, we had many different ideas: at one point we even thought he should have fins. But it was perhaps too fantastical and we settled for realistic touches and things like 'he prefers not to shake hands'. In the original script, Jaws was a lot scarier and a lot more vicious. Lewis Gilbert perceived that there should be an element of humour in what Jaws was doing. That's why we added the bit where Jaws drops the giant rock on his foot at the end of the Pyramid sequence. That's clearly when we told the audience: there's an element of fun to the character. The menace was there but there was something almost endearing about him. Christopher Wood

One of my favourite villains is Stromberg in *The Spy Who Loved Me*; he was smooth, romantic, clever, absolutely ruthless and embodied the definition of what a Bond villain should be. John Glen

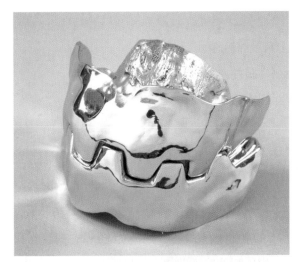

When the character Jaws, played by Richard Kiel in *The Spy Who Loved Me*, came on, I was delighted. What a wonderfully clever thing to do. *Jaws*, both my novel and the film by Steven Spielberg, were big at the time, and to have a character with steel teeth in this giant man was a compliment to the storyteller and to the filmmaker. And I thought he was a great villain. I met him a couple of years later on an airplane and he was a charming man. PETER BENCHLEY

When we did *The Spy Who Loved Me,* I suggested the idea of Jaws being indestructible. That was my main contribution to the character. He was the villain, but the fact that he kept cheating death also made him endearing. And we got a lot of fanmail saying, why can't he be a goodie instead of a baddie? So we brought him back in *Moonraker* and he ended up on Bond's side. LEWIS GILBERT

The films have international appeal because the villains have a global agenda.
For the villain in *GoldenEye*, he had to be a doppelgänger for Bond himself; he is 006,
he is very good looking and in this case, it's like Bond looking into himself.
At the beginning, he is on a mission with Bond, he is apparently executed and then it
turns out that he is alive and is involved with a defection. So *GoldenEye* is sort of
unique that way – we did not have a villain who wants to take over the world,
it was the story of a betrayal by 006. It was a good device. MARTIN CAMPBELL

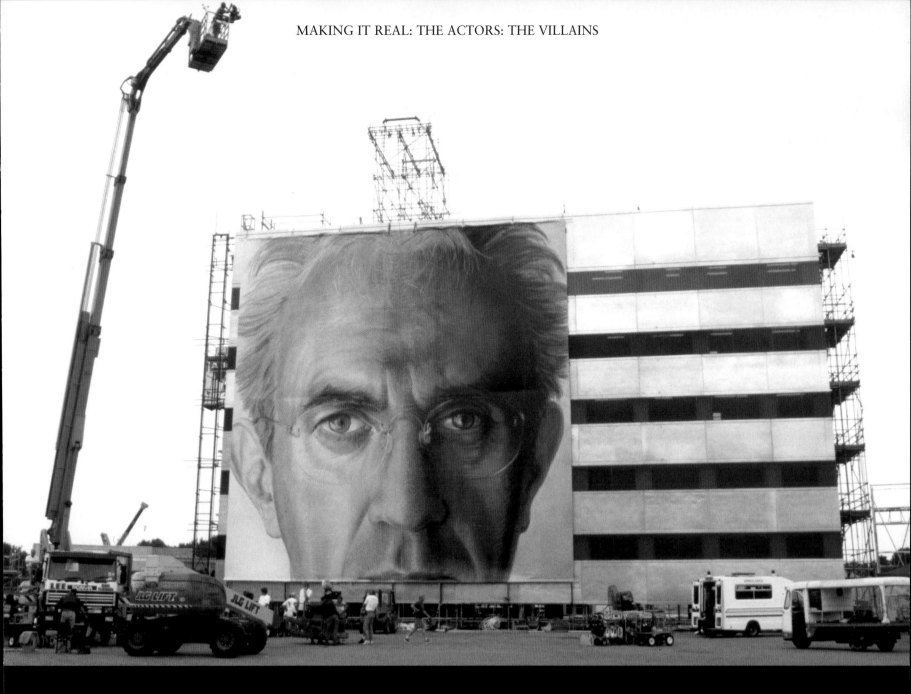

When people find out that you've written a Bond film, they almost immediately say, 'I've got a great idea for a Bond villain: Goldfinger's daughter!' Second in contention is Bill Gates. One of the most interesting things I've found about the cultural impact of Bond is how many actors – and civilians – want to play a Bond villain. I was at a dinner once, where Ron Silver and Tony Curtis both cornered me and asked about playing a villain. But the funniest was taking my kids to a Wiggles concert – they're a group of four incredibly sweet guys who are currently the world's biggest kids' entertainers – and sure enough,

when we met them backstage and they found out I was a Bond writer, they said, 'We want to be Bond villains!' I wanted Elliott Carver in *Tomorrow Never Dies* to be a larger-than-life villain. He is someone who can do anything that is possible to do today with an unlimited amount of money. And I was in my hotel room, flipping channels one morning between different news networks watching their coverage of the Israeli/Palestinian conflict, and getting two very different takes on the same story. And it stuck with me. At that moment, I thought the villain would be in the media. BRUCE FEIRSTEIN

The key to any thriller is to have a good villain and I was very lucky with *The World Is Not Enough* because I immediately thought that Renard was a great character; I loved the fact that he does not feel pain, that a bullet is in his brain and slowly killing him. I remember at one point, someone suggested, what if he can't feel pleasure either, so that added dimension to the character. But what was truly unique was that we purposely misled the audience into believing that Renard was the chief villain and then revealed that Elektra, the love interest, was really behind it all. It was a great twist. MICHAEL APTED

I loved working on the character of Zao, Graves's henchman in *Die Another Day*. He is a great villain who is traded in for Bond at the beginning of the story and now this maniac is out in the world. It's insulting to Bond and he needs to get him; it's a personal vendetta. Zao is prepared to have his bone marrow killed off to become the thing that he hates the most, a Westerner. But James Bond comes in and interrupts the treatment. The idea for the diamond shrapnel in his face came about because a friend told me he was in a car accident when he was a kid; he went through the windshield and even though he is now in his forties, he still has bits of glass working their way out. So we took that and incorporated it in the Zao character. ROBERT WADE

The idea for Graves, the villain in *Die Another Day*, is somewhat based on the character Drax from *Moonraker*, the novel. In the book, he is a Nazi who had his face reconstructed. So that's where the idea of the villain getting a new identity came about. LEE TAMAHORI

Debbie McWilliams, our casting director, is always looking for great faces and she found Mads Mikkelsen to play Le Chiffre, and he is absolutely perfect for the role. Le Chiffre means 'cipher' – you don't know what he is, the man is like a ghost but he is a brilliant card player and essentially Bond has to go up against him. MARTIN CAMPBELL

Sebastien Foucan, who plays Mollaka in *Casino Royale*, is an extraordinary athlete. It's amazing how he could run, jump and feel so free in any environment, no matter what the obstacles were. ALEXANDER WITT

In *Casino Royale*, we made a very deliberate attempt not to make the villains stand out as such. It's very hard not to dress a villain in a dark suit and for Le Chiffre, we decided to do something very simple, luxurious and minimalist. He is almost Bond's alter ego – he should be able to move into any society at any time. Mainly, the audience should focus on his face and his body language. LINDY HEMMING

One of the nice things with Bond is that you have certain characters like Bond himself, M, Moneypenny and Q, that you don't really have to introduce to the audience. We've seen them in the previous films, but what you must do is develop them with each new picture. *Goldfinger* was the first time I worked with Desmond Llewelyn, who played Q. As an actor, he was always very nervous about his lines but I remember when we shot his scene with Bond, he practically got on his knees! I said to him, 'What are you doing? You hate the man! He pays no attention to what you say about your wonderful toys, he always uses them in the wrong way and for the wrong reasons and he never returns them to you! He spoils everything.' And from then on, we developed a character out of Q. With Miss Moneypenny and Lois Maxwell, when we got to *Diamonds Are Forever*, I thought we must get her out of the office. So we managed to cook up a scene where Bond is at the border posing as someone else and she shows up as a customs officer and they have this really nice exchange. With Bernard Lee as M, getting him out of that office was more difficult because I thought, that's where he lives! GUY HAMILTON

I wanted to embrace the scenes with Moneypenny. They're some of the best love scenes in the films. There's also a great kick when Q comes in. That's something to look forward to when you watch the films. Desmond Llewelyn was so much part of the fabric. Everyone loved him. It was wonderful meeting him on *GoldenEye*. MARTIN CAMPBELL

For a long time Q was my favourite character in the Bond films; he was never present enough for my taste. I loved the fact that he would always scold Bond and I used to look forward to seeing Q coming in with a sour face, already angry that James was not going to bring back his toys in one piece. The humour in those scenes was great. STEVEN SPIELBERG

M, Q, Moneypenny, even the different actors playing Felix Leiter... They were all quite good in their own field. Those were also very good parts that everybody remembered – it is not often that actors get the opportunity of playing such memorable parts.
It is common on television, but not in movies. LEWIS GILBERT

When Neal and I were writing *Die Another Day*, we decided we did not want to have the normal Moneypenny moment. So we came up with showing Moneypenny dead and then revealing that it's a virtual training exercise. ROBERT WADE

And during filming we were asked to create another moment and show Bond and Moneypenny making love, until we realize that Moneypenny is using the virtual goggles. And that got a huge laugh; the audience loved it. NEAL PURVIS

With that particular scene, we knew we were tinkering with history but as long as it was an illusion, we could get away with it. LEE TAMAHORI

On *GoldenEye*, Martin Campbell said to me,
'What do you think we should do about the scenes with M?
Let's try her as a woman.' BRUCE FEIRSTEIN

Our instinct was if we were going to cast M as a woman, we needed to find an actress who could be totally believable and not cartoonish. Our fear was that it would be laughable and the big thing was to get someone of the calibre of Judi Dench to play the role. And because M is the only authoritative figure in Bond's life, the casting of a woman as M gave the relationship a whole new dimension. BARBARA BROCCOLI

M was a man for so many years, it took a bit of convincing to switch to a woman. Originally, I was going to cast someone younger. And the head of the studio, John Calley, said,

'You need a star! You need someone with an incredible screen presence, how about Judi Dench?' MARTIN CAMPBELL

Judi Dench is an amazing actress and Pierce was very much aware of it, and he kept saying, give me more stuff to do with her. So we beefed up her character in *The World Is Not Enough* but it became a big challenge. I remember the moment where we were sitting around tossing ideas and we thought, maybe she could be kidnapped. And we went, oh that's ridiculous and then we realized, why not? It was a bold idea but what was great was that Michael and Barbara did not shy away from it. I remember being on the set and just watching Robert Carlisle, who played Renard, working with Judi Dench and thinking, those are two of the greatest actors in Britain and they're acting together in a very well-written scene. I thought, we're doing some really good work here. MICHAEL APTED

Judi Dench playing M was a brilliant piece of casting. She had to dress for MI6 so there's restriction to what she can wear. On *Casino Royale*, we decided to go a bit more sexy. Fortunately for us, Mr Armani had produced a very nice collection of slightly vampy suits in very dark colours. We then allowed a little lace to show here and there. She even had red silk pajamas when she is in bed. And Judi Dench just loved doing this. LINDY HEMMING

Casino Royale doesn't start with the iconic image of the gun barrel. It comes a bit later and is actually part of a scene. Rather than having it as an abstract white background, it's the setting of one of the killings through which Bond wins his double-O status. NEAL PURVIS

The opening sequence of *Casino Royale* goes back to Ian Fleming's novel, although the killings portrayed in the book are slightly different. But the idea was to show that killing is not something that Bond enjoys doing, but it's something he is good at. ROBERT WADE

Making It Real: the opening sequences

No Bond film would be complete without a pre-credit sequence. We always look back at the one from *Goldfinger* as being perfect, and as being the ultimate one to emulate. In those few first minutes, you get an idea of what Bond's life is like on a daily basis. It's like a mini movie. And that's really when the tradition of creating a pre-title sequence really began. Barbara Broccoli

Casino Royale opens with two different kills – one that takes place in a bathroom. It's very violent, very messy. And the other is a straight kill with a gun in an office. There's no slapstick humour. The actual energy is very different from what we've seen before. Gary Powell

One of my favourite pre-credit sequences is in *On Her Majesty's Secret Service*. It was quite challenging because we needed to introduce George Lazenby as the new Bond. So, you have a big fight scene where Bond saves the woman and she runs out on him, and then he looks directly into the camera and says, 'This never happened to the other fellow.' That was wonderful, it was a wink to the audience but it also meant there are no rules, be prepared for the unexpected. JOHN GLEN

When I was working with screenwriter Roald Dahl on the script for *You Only Live Twice*, we were trying to come up with something original for the pre-credit sequence. It was a challenge because there was nothing in the book to draw from and then we just said, what about killing Bond? We then fleshed out the idea with the funeral at sea, the body being picked up by frogmen and brought on board a submarine... And then you realize Bond is still alive. Everyone, including Sean, liked it. We never expected the audience to really believe that Bond was dead but it was something different and daring. LEWIS GILBERT

BRITISH NAVAL COMMANDER MURDERED

In the early hours of this morning, in an Hong Kong Hotel bedroom, was discovered the body of the British Naval Commander James Bond.

The body was discovered by two Police Inspectors of the Hong Kong Police Force, who answered an emergency call from a nearby bar. The gunfire was heard by people in the street below, and the police were on the scene within minutes.

As yet there has been no arrest made, but the police are working on a definite clue. Foul play is suspected and the question is being asked what a high ranking naval officer was doing in such a notorious district.

Bond films were the forerunner of action films. Even the opening sequences always had some alarming stunts that had never been attempted before – my absolute favourite is the one from *The Spy Who Loved Me*. I think it's the best Bond opening ever. MARTIN CAMPBELL

One of the most spectacular pre-credit sequences was in *The Spy Who Loved Me*, where you have a ski chase, Bond jumps off a cliff and his parachute opens. JOHN GLEN

We were prepping *The Spy Who Loved Me*, and I remember Michael Wilson showing me an ad in *Playboy* with this guy on skis, jumping off a cliff. We brought him in and we found out that the picture was a fake; it was a mock-up. But he said, I know where and how to do it for real. LEWIS GILBERT

I went down to a preview of *The Spy Who Loved Me* in Westwood, California with both Cubby and Rick Sylvester. At that point, Rick had not seen the scene cut together and when he did, I remember him saying, 'Holy sh–!' TOM MANKIEWICZ

The guy's name was Rick Sylvester and he wanted to do the jump from Mount Asgard in the Arctic Circle. So I went up there with my crew and I could not believe it. When we arrived it was perfect but we were not ready to film and once we got into position, the weather became awful and it stayed that way for about three weeks. Back in London, they were all nervous about the time and money that were being spent just waiting for the weather to change. But I felt I had to have perfect conditions to do the shot. Finally, one morning, the helicopter pilot said, 'I think you might be lucky today.' And it took us about an hour and a half to get into position and we did the shot. Rick skied off the cliff and was illuminated by the sun as he went down; it was beautiful and we had the shot in the bag before we even started principal photography on the film. I believe that it was that particular shot that eventually led me to be asked to direct *For Your Eyes Only* a few years later. It was an audacious image. Originally, we were going to have both the British and the Russian flag on Bond's parachute, since the film was about the two nations working together.

But the idea was lost and we just went with the statement of the British flag. JOHN GLEN

187

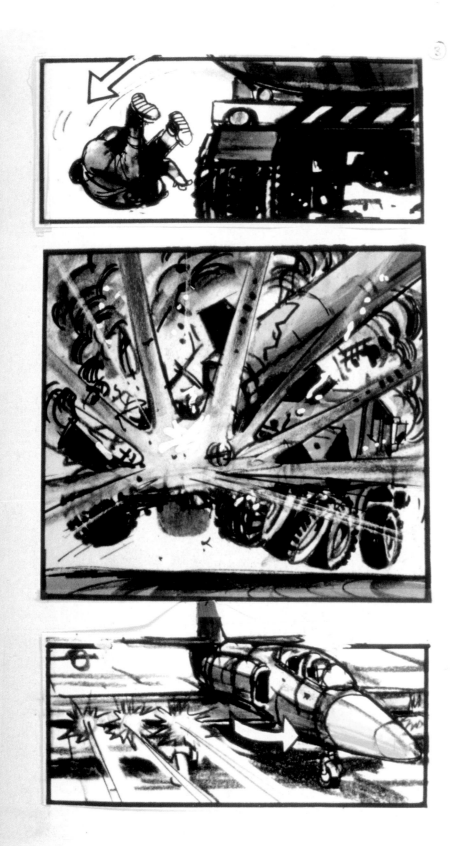

For the opening sequence of *Tomorrow Never Dies*, the challenge was to find the location, a runway in a mountainous region. It's supposed to take place in Afghanistan, and the great thing about Bond is that the producers have connections with location managers all over the world. So we got a call about this place in the Pyrenees and it was perfect. It was close to a ski resort, so we had easy road access. But the scene had to take place in the snow, and of course it was melting. So my art directors had the problem of trucking snow in. The most interesting thing for me was that the director Roger Spottiswoode wanted a Russian rocket launcher. We managed to bring one that was decommissioned from Moscow and drove it all the way across Europe to our location. I'll never forget seeing this gigantic machine coming up the road; it was quite extraordinary. ALLAN CAMERON

For me, designing the opening sequences for Bond is coming up with something nobody else ever thought of, nobody ever dared to do. By the time we got onto *Tomorrow Never Dies*, everything had been done. So we said, let's just give the audience a big 'shoot 'em up'! We knew the action had to be centred around an arms deal – we threw in jet planes and designed a big action sequence. We basically decided that we were not going to have a single scene, but a montage of everything we could think of. It was planned meticulously and it took two weeks to shoot it. Vic Armstrong

On *The World Is Not Enough*, I thought that the Guggenheim in Bilbao sequence, with Bond's escape through a window after a shoot-out, was good enough for a pre-title sequence. But when I previewed the film, the audience was not satisfied. I immediately said, let's compress the Bilbao part and combine it with the chase on the Thames, which was originally placed right after the opening credits. When you do a Bond film, you must have a stand-up prologue and what I had done was against the instinct of the tradition; I had a mediocre prologue and a stand-up action scene following the titles. And thank God we previewed the film! MICHAEL APTED

The chase in the opening scene of *The World Is Not Enough* was filmed on different parts of the Thames and climaxed at the dome which was under construction for the Millennium. The hot-air balloon exploding was a miniature, filmed separately, so there were a lot of different elements, conceived by everyone – including our second-unit director Vic Armstrong. PETER LAMONT

For *Die Another Day*, Neal Purvis and I came up with ending the pre-credit sequence with Bond *not* getting himself out of trouble. He is captured and thrown in jail. It was a controversial departure but everyone went for it. It gave the film a great set-up.

ROBERT WADE

One of the most exciting Bond fights was at the beginning of *Thunderball* between Bond and an assassin who disguised himself as a woman. And that fight was really accomplished with tremendous cutting; the editing in that sequence was very clever. Sometimes they would speed up the action, or they would remove a few frames and it just pulled you into the action in a way that I had never before seen in a choreographed, staged fight. And I love how the fight ends, when Bond throws the flowers on the body of the guy before he leaves the room. I also remember being blown away by that very clever, hand-to-hand combat between Sean Connery and Robert Shaw in the train car in *From Russia With Love*. That was one of the most exciting fights I had ever witnessed as a movie lover. And later on, I had a chance to discuss that scene with both Robert Shaw when I directed him in *Jaws* and Sean Connery when we did *Indiana Jones and the Last Crusade*. STEVEN SPIELBERG

We're so intimately involved with the creation of the screenplay, the assembling of the crew and the selection of the cast that once you actually start shooting, it becomes the director's movie. We're around and we're on the set every day but it is a director's medium. We have certain parameters that are dictated by the history of the films, but once the blueprint is done, it's only right that the director should just go ahead and do it. We usually have a five-, six-month pre-production so by the time we start shooting, we're all on the same page. And the excitement is to see how the director visualizes it. BARBARA BROCCOLI

The filming itself was always very well organized. For instance, I would never attempt a stunt until I knew it was ready to be done. Pre-planning on Bond films was a big thing. All the different departments got involved early on and worked very hard at making sure everything was perfect before we started filming. And we never went over schedule. GUY HAMILTON

In 1969, I was at my father's farm and the phone rang. Someone explained how I was on a flight the next day to Switzerland to do *On Her Majesty's Secret Service*. George Leech was the co-ordinator on the film and I ended up doubling George Lazenby in some of the scenes; I was involved in the fight on the bobsleigh run, in the attack at the end where I jumped out of a helicopter, the car chase, the fight in the barn with all the bells, the end of the ski chase where Bond hangs over a cliff, and parts of the cable-car sequence. We had a great team: there was Luggi Leitner, who was a phenomenal skier, and we had Willy Bogner who could ski backwards while holding the camera... For years, a lot of people said that *On Her Majesty's Secret Service* had the best action sequences ever in a Bond film. VIC ARMSTRONG

Bob Simmons was a wonderful stunt co-ordinator – he was very good at the choreography of the action scenes. My job really was to make sure we got it all on film. On a Bond film, it's a collaboration between everybody; even Sean Connery had ideas when it came to stunts and action scenes. LEWIS GILBERT

We had some great action sequences in *Live And Let Die*. One of them involved a double-decker bus going underneath a bridge that was too short and that would cut off the top deck. We first had to find the right bridge and then built the bus with the top deck mounted on a rail so it could slide off easily. There was also a spectacular motorboat chase sequence. One of the boats had to go fifteen feet up in the air and designing that scene was done purely through trial and error. We knew the stunt had to be done for real. I built a ramp and we kept trying with different boats; we destroyed about twenty-four of them. In the end, we had to redesign a boat to make the stunt work. SYD CAIN

When I was directing *Diamonds Are Forever*, I'd seen on television a French stunt driver who drove a car around an airfield and suddenly had it up on two wheels; I thought it was tremendously impressive. So we tried to think of that in Bondian terms and came up with the idea of a car chase that ended up in an alleyway that got too narrow, and we thought it would be great to have Bond's car go through it up on two wheels and have the other vehicle

Filming action scenes with animals… In *Live And Let Die*, we had crocodiles and snakes. The snake in the bathroom sequence for instance where Bond is shaving, was the best snake I ever worked with in my entire career! It poked its head out, had a look, went down the pipe slowly and all in one take. Brilliant. But then we got to the scene where Geoffrey Holder, who played Baron Samedi, had to fall into a coffin full of snakes. He hated snakes and refused to do it. Luckily, on that day, the former King of Greece came to visit the set and poor Geoffrey thought he might create a bad publicity incident and went ahead with the scene. GUY HAMILTON

In *The Man With The Golden Gun*, the plot dictated for Bond to be driving on one side of a canal, and Scaramanga on the other. We found a good spot to do the stunt – but because the car had to go up in the air from one side, flip and end up on the other side, some serious calculations were involved. We needed a ramp to be at a certain degree, the car had to go at a certain speed and so on. The challenge in the design was that it had to look like a wrecked bridge and yet, it had to be strong enough to sustain the car. We were all expecting to do that shot two or three times, but it worked on take one and we all went home early that day. PETER MURTON

One of my favourite action sequences is in *Licence To Kill*, where Bond takes his spear gun and shoots into the float of an airplane, gets towed along, and is waterskiing barefoot. That entire sequence came to be because someone walked into the office one day and said: 'Barefoot waterskiing.' It's a wonderful scene because it's all about getting out of an impossible situation through improvisation. But the most intense, the most prolonged action scene in not only the history of Bond but probably in film history, was the truck chase sequence. I developed it over a long period of time. I filmed it first with the principals for three days. Remy Julienne and his team did all the stunts. JOHN GLEN

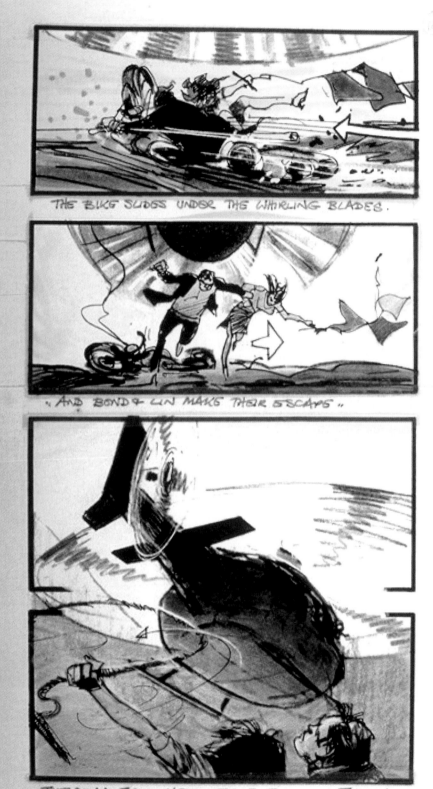

THE BIKE SLIDES UNDER THE WHIRLING BLADES.

"AND BOND & LIN MAKE THEIR ESCAPE"

TILT DOWN FROM HELICOPTER TO FIND LIN TWIRLING
THE WASHING LINE

For the motorcycle chase sequence in *Tomorrow Never Dies*, Roger Spottiswoode wanted it to go across rooftops. I visited several locations in Vietnam but we could not find a place that had rooftops that could accommodate the stunts we had in mind. We ended up in Bangkok and found three big tenement blocks with flat roofs on the first day we arrived. We had to reinforce the structure of the houses and later, we also built portions of the streets on a backlot in England. All those different elements combined made for a fantastic scene. The jump of the motorcycle over the helicopter was yet another challenge. We had 7,000 cardboard boxes and mattresses so that the motorcycle could land safely. We practised and rehearsed the stunt for two weeks. It was all done very safely, using the real body of a helicopter. VIC ARMSTRONG

Chris Corbould and his effects team created the helicopter. It was real except it had no blades; they were added later on thanks to computer graphics. But this scene is a good example of working closely with all the different departments. ALLAN CAMERON

At the time of *GoldenEye*, I remember that the British press particularly was down on reviving Bond. But I thought, the hell with it. Let's just make the film! And Barbara and Michael just let me get on with it. In terms of the look of the film and the discussions I had with my director of photography Phil Meheux, we realized that all the Bond films have a gloss to them. So on *GoldenEye*, it was important to maintain the look established in the previous Bond films. I had Simon Crane as stunt co-ordinator and he was amazing. But I must also say that the real secret to a lot of the action sequences in *GoldenEye* is Derek Meddings, who was the miniature effects supervisor – he died shortly after finishing the film and *GoldenEye* is dedicated to him. He was a genius. There are a lot of models in the film: the train, the helicopter, the giant radio telescope at the end... and Derek made it all look real. MARTIN CAMPBELL

I've always loved the classic image of Douglas Fairbanks Sr in *The Black Pirate*, plunging a knife into a sail and riding down while hanging on the knife's hilt as the sail splits. I thought it would be great to do something similar when Bond and the girl jump off a building in *Tomorrow Never Dies*. I was in Hong Kong and I saw buildings under construction, with scaffolding covered with advertising billboards. Suddenly I got the idea of combining the *Black Pirate* image with the billboards in Hong Kong. And to add insult to injury, the billboard was the face of Carver, the villain. So on their way down, Bond and the girl basically rip off his face. VIC ARMSTRONG

STRAIGHT ONTO BANNER - TILT DOWN WITH THE FALLING COUPLE - LETTING THEM EXIT FRAME

CUTAWAY TO BOND STRUGGLING TO RETAIN HIS GRIP,,

In *Die Another Day*, I feared that the fencing sequence would be boring to watch. In a Bond film, that type of scene has very little juice. So, I decided to build the sequence up and to have Bond and the villain go at it with sabres, with broadswords and so on. Everyone embraced the concept, and we had Bob Anderson, the king of all sword-fight scenes, working with us. The sequence ended up being much larger and more exciting than I thought. Also, we did not know what to do at the end of the film. Where should Bond and Jinx be? And I thought, they have a helicopter full of diamonds, let's evoke the Sixties Bond films, and let's have them in a room with the diamonds. With the last scene, what you want is a quiet moment with Bond and the girl. LEE TAMAHORI

On *The World Is Not Enough*, for me, it was about keeping action sequences as realistic as possible. Although there is a fantasy element to the action scenes, at the core there is reality. The most important thing I discovered was how much attention I had to pay to the two or sometimes three other units. I not only had to watch my 'dailies' – that is, the scenes that were shot the previous day – but I had to watch the footage from the other units. Keeping track of everything was the biggest challenge and I was very lucky to be working with the best possible crew. MICHAEL APTED

CONTINUE TILT DOWN - BOND & LIN FALL THRU' AND OUT OF FRAME..

TOP SHOT, EXT. BUILDING - THEY ARE BROUGHT TO A JERKING HALT AS THE BANNER RUNS OUT.

Initially, after I read the first draft of *Casino Royale*, I thought it was going to be an easy film. But it kept evolving and growing and it turned into one of the biggest action films I've ever done. For example, there's a complicated chase that includes 'free running' through a construction site; there's an action scene at an airport between a tanker and a tow-truck with a huge explosion, and at the end of the film, you have a sinking house in Venice. CHRIS CORBOULD

On *Casino Royale*, we did a scene at a construction site and it was all done for real. There was no CGI involved. But it was a very dangerous environment because it was very easy to lose your balance. The sequence involves Bond and a villain who is very agile; he is a free-style runner who goes very fast, and the way he runs is almost like a ballet. To realize the sequence, we used an unfinished building in the Bahamas and we brought in the girders and the cranes. It took about five to six weeks to realize the sequence and it ended up being about five minutes of on-screen time. ALEXANDER WITT

The sinking house at the end of *Casino Royale* involved the biggest hydraulic rig I've ever dealt with in my career. It was massive and was mounted on an hydraulic gimbal that could be lowered into water. The weight of it was probably 80 to 90 tons and it was completely controlled by a computer. We would programme in a move and it would replicate it over and over. This was not something I'd ever done before and it was very exciting. CHRIS CORBOULD

Whether the film was finished or not, the new Bond was always set to open on a very specific date at the Odeon Leicester Square. So we worked on a very tight deadline. On *Goldfinger*, the raid on Fort Knox had not worked out so I had to do it all over again with a cameraman at the last minute. And we literally had four weeks to edit. It was a rush to get the film to the theatre on time. GUY HAMILTON

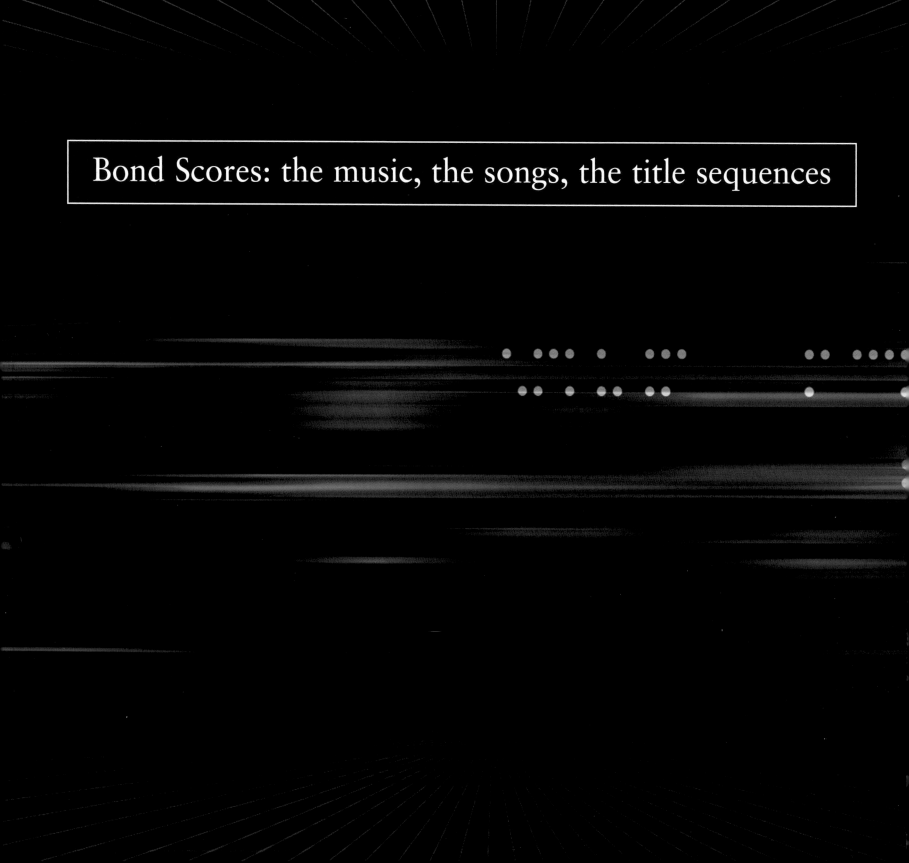

Bond Scores: the music, the songs, the title sequences

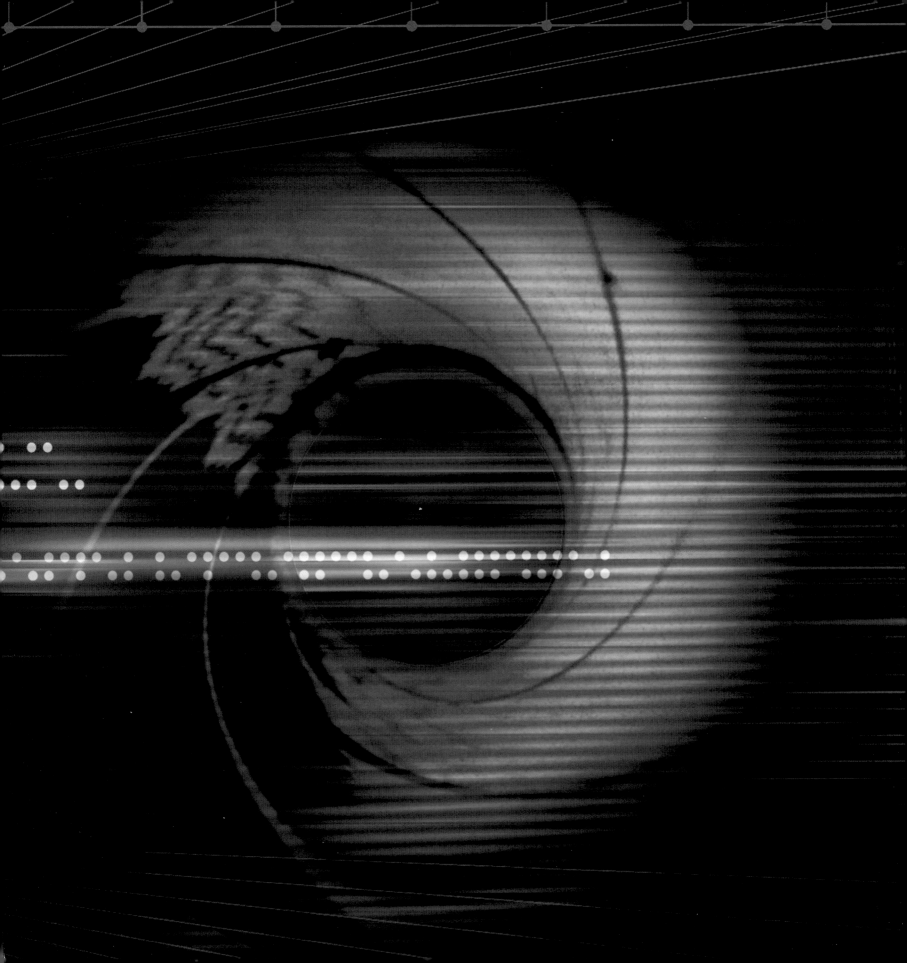

I have been an admirer of John Barry for many years. All of his music stands the test of time and he is one of the best composers of film scores. I love *The Quiller Memorandum, The Ipcress Files, The Lion in Winter, Out Of Africa* and many others. But above all, John Barry will be revered for his contribution to the Bond series. And it's not just his composition of the main title themes, but also his underscoring. When I hear the underscoring to his Bond movies, it doesn't matter who is playing Bond because the mortar that holds the different styles of brick together is the music. Usually a film score follows behind the action but in the case of John Barry, it feels like the music came first and the action second. STEVEN SPIELBERG

There's a gentleman called Noel Rogers who used to be head of publishing with United Artists Music in London, terrific guy, terrific music man and he was the one who went to Harry and Cubby and recommended me. I recorded the music with my band, the John Barry Seven – that's how it started. JOHN BARRY

John Barry's themes and style are very distinctive and set the whole tone for the films. The music is a very important aspect of the film. When we use the theme in a trailer announcing the next Bond, audiences immediately become excited. MICHAEL G. WILSON

John Barry is part of the DNA of the Bond world. Bond is a solitary character and you have to find ways to give him an identity through different things, and music is one of them. BARBARA BROCCOLI

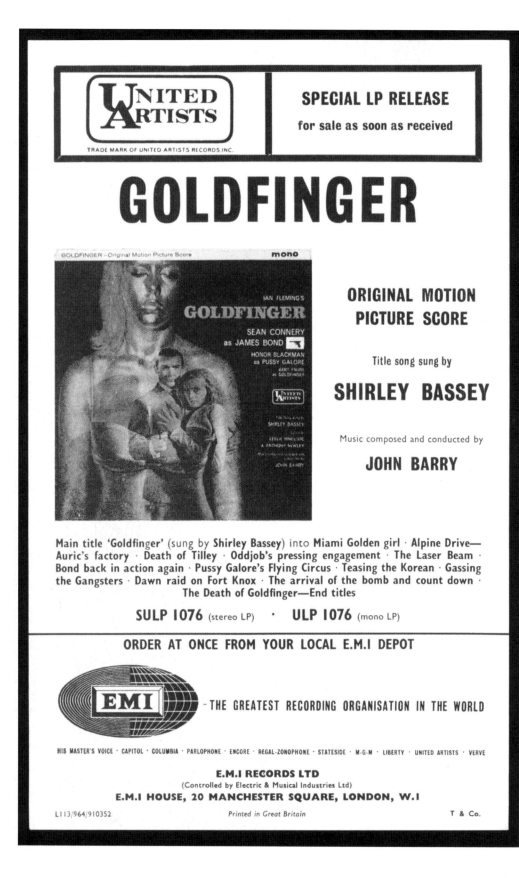

UNITED ARTISTS
TRADE MARK OF UNITED ARTISTS RECORDS,INC.

SPECIAL LP RELEASE
for sale as soon as received

GOLDFINGER

GOLDFINGER – Original Motion Picture Score   mono

IAN FLEMING'S
GOLDFINGER
SEAN CONNERY
as JAMES BOND
HONOR BLACKMAN
as PUSSY GALORE

ORIGINAL MOTION
PICTURE SCORE

Title song sung by

SHIRLEY BASSEY

Music composed and conducted by

JOHN BARRY

Main title 'Goldfinger' (sung by Shirley Bassey) into Miami Golden girl · Alpine Drive—Auric's factory · Death of Tilley · Oddjob's pressing engagement · The Laser Beam · Bond back in action again · Pussy Galore's Flying Circus · Teasing the Korean · Gassing the Gangsters · Dawn raid on Fort Knox · The arrival of the bomb and count down · The Death of Goldfinger—End titles

SULP 1076 (stereo LP)   ·   ULP 1076 (mono LP)

ORDER AT ONCE FROM YOUR LOCAL E.M.I DEPOT

EMI –THE GREATEST RECORDING ORGANISATION IN THE WORLD

HIS MASTER'S VOICE · CAPITOL · COLUMBIA · PARLOPHONE · ENCORE · REGAL-ZONOPHONE · STATESIDE · M.G.M · LIBERTY · UNITED ARTISTS · VERVE

E.M.I RECORDS LTD
(Controlled by Electric & Musical Industries Ltd)
E.M.I HOUSE, 20 MANCHESTER SQUARE, LONDON, W.I

L113/964/910352   Printed in Great Britain   T & Co.

After *Dr No* the next film was *From Russia With Love* and they wanted Lional Bart to do the song and me to do the score. But when *Goldfinger* came up, I said, I want to do the whole thing and I want to integrate the song into the score. I called Shirley Bassey, who was huge at the time, particularly in England. I remember her first question was, 'What's *Goldfinger*?' I said, 'Look, don't worry about it, don't intellectualize it too much.' The song was written by Anthony Newley and Leslie Bricusse. I loved the lyrics, words like 'the Midas touch' were brilliant, it was so simple. I had four trumpets, five trombones, a tuba and four French horns. So you got that great Wagnerian-like sound at the beginning of the song. The movie opened and the song went to number one. So that was really the beginning for me. Of all the Bond scores I did, *Goldfinger* remains my favourite. And after *Goldfinger*, we would literally look at the hit parade to choose a singer for the next film. JOHN BARRY

When you start a Bond film, people are always asking: 'Who is playing James Bond? Who is the villain? What car is he driving? Who is the girl? And who is singing the song?' The song is a big part of the films. BARBARA BROCCOLI

Shirley Bassey singing 'Goldfinger' is the iconic identifier of the entire series. When you hear that song, you immediately know who Bond is. However, my all-time favourite Bond song is 'Live and Let Die' by Paul McCartney. STEVEN SPIELBERG

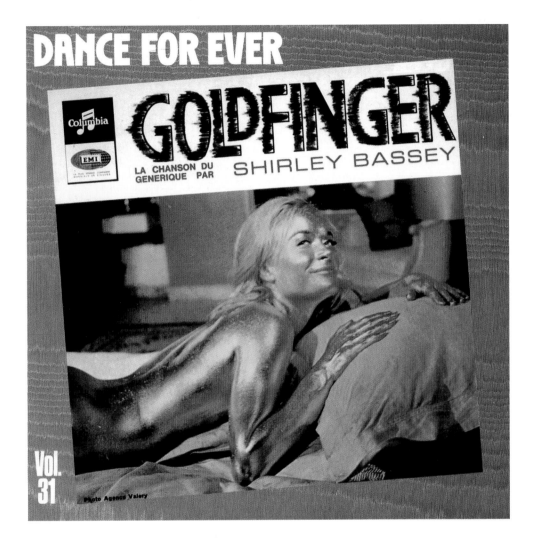

When we did *Goldfinger*, I was already a great fan of John Barry. But I had very little to do with the music because John was in such a rush to produce it. I didn't really hear anything until the last minute. GUY HAMILTON

Some movies don't necessarily lend themselves to a song but the Bond films do. The great fun was to come up with suggestive lyrics. It was the Sixties and those things were allowed. The song set the tone, that tongue-in-cheek feeling, the double entendres – it was part of the whole thing. When we got to *Thunderball*, I remember I had seen a piece in a newspaper saying that the Italians had nicknamed James Bond, 'Mr Kiss Kiss Bang Bang'. And I thought that would be a great title for the song for the film and we recorded it with Dionne Warwick. But we ended up with another song that used the title of the film – and it was a difficult title to use in the lyrics. The producers always preferred a song with the title of the movie and rightly so because each time the song played on the radio, it was free advertising for the film. JOHN BARRY

It was fun to have John Barry not only do the score but also do a cameo appearance in *The Living Daylights*. He wanted to play the conductor. He'll live forever through his music so having him on film as well was amazing. JOHN GLEN

There is the Bond Theme but there's also the 007 Theme, which John Barry created for *From Russia With Love*. There's a sense of expectation in it. There's something starting and stopping, but you don't quite know when it's going to happen. It's also quite joyous and it works because it has a simple yet immediately memorable and identifiable melody. DAVID ARNOLD

The Bond Theme was very dramatic and I felt that it needed some opening up. That's when I wrote the 007 Theme. It was a larger kind of lyrical moment and it was perfect for *From Russia With Love*. I also used it in *Thunderball*, *You Only Live Twice*, *Diamonds Are Forever* and *Moonraker*. It was a big open melody and there was a sense of fun about it, as opposed to the Bond Theme, which was serious and moody. The 007 Theme covered a spacious kind of mood. But when George Lazenby was cast to replace Sean Connery in *On Her Majesty's Secret Service*, I went back to the Bond Theme. My goal was to make him as Bondian as possible through the music. I used synthesizers to give an electronic edge to the score and it was very powerful. JOHN BARRY

The ending of *On Her Majesty's Secret Service* is a good example of the power of John Barry's music. We end the film with the killing of Bond's wife and it's really the music that gets you out of that dark moment. JOHN GLEN

With *On Her Majesty's Secret Service*, we decided to have a song in a montage sequence where Bond falls in love and we selected Louis Armstrong. What inspired me to think of him was his beautiful song 'What a Wonderful World'. He'd been very ill for about a year and we went to America because he couldn't travel.

We only did two or three takes and he was unbelievable. I loved the way he said the word 'world'. He was a true gentleman. JOHN BARRY

[I remember] Cubby calling me and asking if he could use the five notes that John Williams had composed for *Close Encounters of the Third Kind* in *Moonraker*. He explained it was going to be the combination on a door. I immediately gave him permission. Then I asked him if he'd changed his mind about me directing a Bond film someday and he said: 'Let me think about it.' And I never heard back from him until the day I called him asking if I could use the James Bond Theme in *The Goonies*, a film I was producing. We had this character named Data who, very much like Q, created amazing little gadgets and gizmos. And Richard Donner, who directed the film, wanted to use the James Bond Theme on a ghetto blaster that hung around Data's neck. When I called Cubby and asked for permission, he immediately said 'no'. And I said, 'but Cubby, you called me a few years ago and asked for permission to use the five notes from *Close Encounters* and I said "yes".' And his response to that was, 'Yes you did, but the James Bond Theme has more than five notes! Which five notes would you like to use?' Then I realized he was only joking and he gave me permission to use the James Bond Theme in *The Goonies*. STEVEN SPIELBERG

We have been lucky with other composers like Marvin Hamlisch, who was a terrific choice for *The Spy Who Loved Me* – I'll never forget him coming into the studio, apologizing for his voice and singing at the piano 'Nobody Does It Better'. There was no doubt it was going to be a hit. JOHN GLEN

Bill Conti did the score for *For Your Eyes Only,* and for the first time we decided to include the song artist, in this case Sheena Easton, in the opening title sequence. It became the first Bond music video. On *Licence To Kill* we had Michael Kamen, who sadly passed away in 2003. In both cases, we got completely different scores, yet the composers managed to maintain the feel established by John Barry. John Glen

The Spy Who Loved Me is my favourite of the three Bond films I directed. I love the humour in it and I think it has the best song, 'Nobody Does It Better' – in fact, the title of the song has become a password for so many things you still hear in commercials today. I also liked to use music as comic relief. In *The Spy Who Loved Me,* we used the score of *Lawrence of Arabia* when Bond and Triple X are walking through the desert. In *Moonraker,* we had the famous opening cue from *2001: A Space Odyssey* during the hunting scene with Drax and we used the tune from *Close Encounters of the Third Kind* as a secret door code. Lewis Gilbert

I have an absolutely vivid recollection of my first experience with Bond. I was eight years old and I had watched the first three movies I ever saw in a theatre: *The Wizard of Oz, Oliver!* and *You Only Live Twice*. But I have to say, *You Only Live Twice* was the most powerful experience, beginning with the first five minutes of the film. You had the gun barrel, then a scene in space, then Bond in bed and then he got killed! Hearing the music for the gun barrel, the space music march and the song was unforgettable, and I have a distinct memory of something changing at that point, of having a sense of what I wanted to do. Within weeks of seeing the film, I wrote in an exercise book, 'When I grow up I either want to be an actor or a composer.' As soon as I did the score for *Stargate*, I went to the music department at MGM and told them that Bond was top of my list; I said, 'If there's an occasion where John Barry is not involved, count me in.' Then I made *Independence Day* and won a Grammy award for it. In the meantime, I had decided to produce an album called *Shaken Not Stirred*, using great artists doing some of my favourite Bond songs. I sent some of the tracks to MGM, and they seemed very pleased. Barbara and Michael were too. We met and when they started editing *Tomorrow Never Dies*, they used some of the *Shaken Not Stirred* cues as temp music. And the combination of hearing a new contemporary way of using the heritage of John Barry, convinced them to give me a shot on *Tomorrow Never Dies*. I wanted to do it for the right reason because I have great affection and great respect for what John Barry did. The first thing I did was to score the pre-credit sequence. I played it to the director Roger Spottiswoode with the rough cut of the sequence and it was glorious. Then, I had to wait for more scenes to be filmed and edited and I basically scored the film scene by scene. DAVID ARNOLD

214

For *The World Is Not Enough*, I felt that the band Garbage could exist within the Bond universe. They could be both on Bond's side, or the baddies'. That was a factor in selecting them for the opening title song. As far as the score itself, my favourite cue is Elektra's theme. John Barry's music is very sensual and elegant and the one thing I think we have in common is that slightly dark, twisted sense of yearning, that kind of reaching beyond your grasp. And Elektra's theme sounds romantic but in fact, it's very sad. I also used her theme in the casino scene, which was a way to make the place be about her. Another one of my favourite cues is the one I wrote for Halle Berry's first scene in *Die Another Day*, as she comes out of the water. When I was writing that specific cue, I thought, 'Who is she?', and while the music for that moment is still very romantic, it has a bit of mystery to it. DAVID ARNOLD

It's very hard to express to a composer what you want. It's very useful when you work with a composer who is willing to make changes at the last minute because until you hear the thing laid out against the film, it's very hard to word a constructive opinion. David Arnold was very good at doing roughs on a synthesizer and he would send them to me. David was the first person to see anything; as soon as I had a sequence put together, I'd send it to him and it gave him a decent amount of time to put the score together. MICHAEL APTED

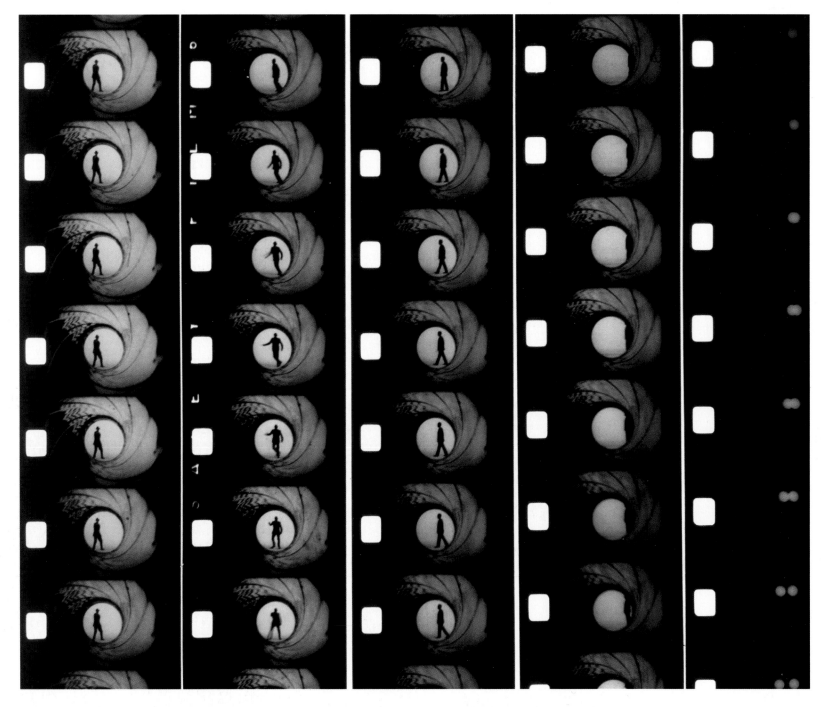

It was Maurice Binder who came up with the gun barrel opening. He was a great artist and designer. His idea was to set the tone and to say to the audience, James Bond is a hunted man and every day of his life, he is in somebody's sights and somebody is trying to kill him. It creates a lot of tension. It also reinforces the fact that the character is a silhouette and that was an element that was very clear in the books. BARBARA BROCCOLI

For years, I never knew it was a gun barrel. The concept is that you're the point of view of the bullet. It's a confusing idea but a very original image which is why it works so well. When I got involved with *GoldenEye*, I decided that one way to revamp it was to give it a three-dimensional effect. I kept the blood coming down but the overall look is a bit shinier.

The main titles on *Dr No* were created by Maurice Binder. The titles for *From Russia With Love* and *Goldfinger* were done by Robert Brownjohn – who was also a very talented artist and did some marvellous, inventive stuff projecting images from the films onto women's figures. Maurice then came back for *Thunderball* with a whole new bag of tricks and worked on all of the subsequent films until he passed away. DAVID CHASMAN

The opening titles set the mood of the movie. But what Maurice Binder and Robert Brownjohn did when they designed the titles for the early Bond films was very experimental. Binder for instance never quite knew how it was going to turn out in the end. He loved to come up with new effects. He'd always start by saying: 'I'd like to work with this substance or texture,' and he'd go from there and experiment with bullets going through water, he'd do things with fire, ice, metal, diamonds. He would be inspired by an element in the film and then he'd play around with it secretly for a long period of time. Then, you'd finally get him to share the process with you. BARBARA BROCCOLI

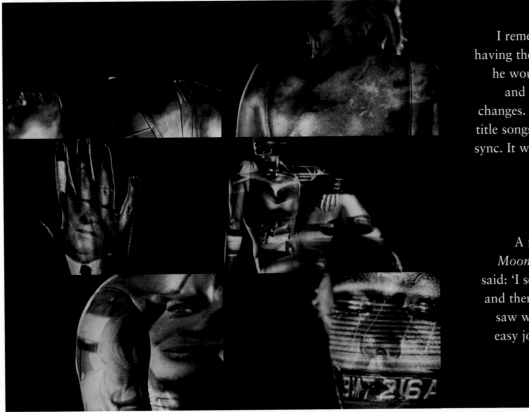

I remember he'd always complain about not having the song to work with. In the early days, he would be using many, many pieces of film and it wasn't as easy as it is today to make changes. Sometimes, he'd get a new mix for the title songs and all of his visuals would be out of sync. It would drive him crazy. MICHAEL G. WILSON

A famous one was when they were doing *Moonraker*, there was a line in the song that said: 'I see your eyes, in a thousands dreams...' and then they changed the beats and what you saw was a lady's rear end. He didn't have an easy job, but he really loved what he did. He was a perfectionist. BARBARA BROCCOLI

Being part of Bond is a childhood fantasy. And the way I ultimately got involved with Bond was when I directed a music video with Gladys Knight for *Licence To Kill*. Because I was a huge fan of Maurice Binder, I approached the music video like a title sequence. Then sadly, between *Licence To Kill* and the next Bond *GoldenEye*, Maurice died, and Barbara and Michael asked me if I'd be interested in doing the title sequence for *GoldenEye*. It was daunting because there's a tradition with the Bond credits. The point was we needed to bring a contemporary feel, it had to be cutting-edge but it had to be familiar. I tried to take on the spirit that Maurice had established. It had to be its own thing but also be a homage to the template that Maurice had created.

With *GoldenEye*, it was like a sequence showing the passing of time. It was a narrative sequence. My favourite image in *GoldenEye* is the big concrete block and a girl in lingerie comes with a hammer and smashes it to pieces. That works graphically and I love the humorous aspect of the idea of communism being brought to its knees by the Western values of girls in lingerie. In terms of the process, I get a script and find out what the main themes are. For instance, on *The World Is Not Enough*, oil was the theme. And that gave me an opportunity to do something different, using black over psychedelic forms and colours. On *Die Another Day*, the narrative element was the strongest it had ever been. In fact, it was scripted. There was a storyline built into the title sequence and that was great. It felt different. But I did try to keep the other elements, like the girls and the sexiness of it.

The way I work is, I do sketches, drawings and storyboards. Sometimes, I do animatics. I do that before the song has been done. I start sharing my ideas with the producers and the director. To build the sequences, we use 3D animation, stock footage, filmed elements. We do casting, we build props and sets. I then edit with a demo track of the song. The actual names and credits are given to me late and I try to use a very simple and very readable font. There's a lot of freedom, it's a collaborative effort and very creative. DANIEL KLEINMAN

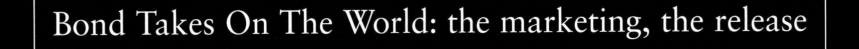

Bond Takes On The World: the marketing, the release

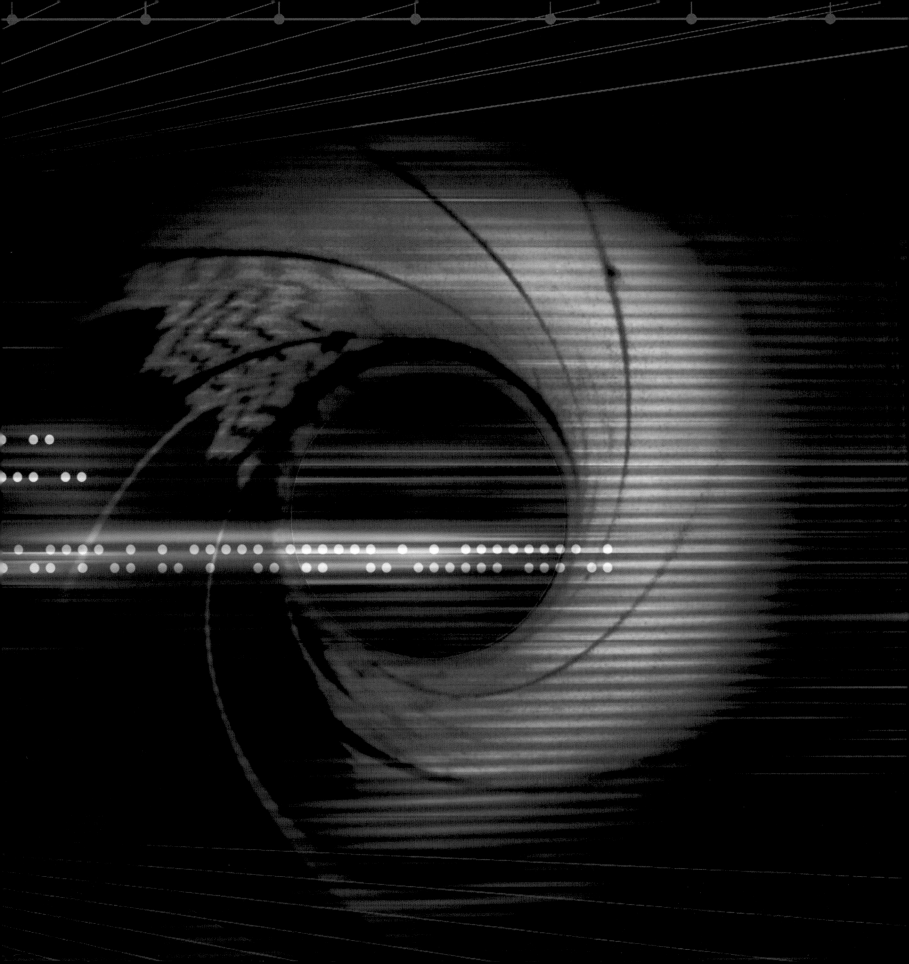

Because Fleming was so finicky about things being the best and good quality, because Bond is always living on the edge, there are certain things that he needs in order to keep himself alive. He needs a car that's not going to let him down, he needs a good watch and so on. Everything he uses on the job has to be the best quality. Fleming describes in great detail all the things that Bond uses, whether it comes down to a glass of wine, a meal he is eating, a car he is driving, or what suit he is wearing. That's how Bond became synonymous with quality goods. That notion really started with the books. If you think you may not be alive tomorrow, you might as well have the best of everything. Therefore, merchandising and promotions have always been integrated activities on Bond. Cubby was the man who created product placement in films. He realized the connection between having products shown in the film and using them to promote the film's release. BARBARA BROCCOLI

The day I was supposed to film the scene where Bond wakes up on Goldfinger's jet and meets Pussy Galore for the first time, I got in early that morning because I wanted to look at the set and check a few things. And to my absolute amazement, there were Fabergé and Gillette products strategically placed on the shelves of the toilets of the plane set. Guy Hamilton

On *Dr No*, I recollect, we did a fairly routine campaign. It was a healthy success, which prompted the second film, *From Russia With Love*. On that one, I took a trip to London, where they were filming it, to do a photo shoot with Sean Connery; that's when the iconic pose of Bond with the pistol alongside his cheek was born, and that was completely improvised. We had a photo session scheduled at the end of a shooting day. When we started, Sean had his jacket on but nobody, including myself, had thought of bringing a pistol. So we had to scramble for one and found an air-pistol which is why, when you study the photograph, it has the long barrel. That photograph was used as a source for a number of drawings that followed and it was also on that occasion that I really got to love Sean Connery. He was amazingly cooperative, and at the end of the session, he said, 'Anyone going to Shepherd's Bush?' I thought that was a very classy thing to ask. In the early- to mid-Sixties, television was a minor advertising tool, it was all print advertising and you worked with basic key art. We introduced several innovations at the time, such as reading the scripts before the pictures were made, so we'd get an idea as to what we wanted to photograph for the campaigns. With Bond, it was obviously glamour, exotic locations and beautiful women, and we got artists like Robert McGinnis, Frank McCarthy, Bob Peaks and Mitchell Hooks to do the posters. We had advertising agencies coming up with ideas, the producers had ideas, I'd come up with concepts and so on. It is impossible to credit any single ad to a single person; it truly became a group effort, a group idea with one exception; the 007 pistol design was entirely the work of designer Joe Caroff.

DAVID CHASMAN

For *Die Another Day*, we wanted to get away from the image of Bond with a woman on either side of him on the poster. We looked at hundreds of concepts. We had special photo shoots. In the US, they have a heavy TV campaign. In other countries, posters are more important. For Japan, we found a young designer in New York who identified a look that was appealing to young audiences and it improved the film's awareness. ANNE BENNETT

DIE ANOTHER DAY

007™

ダイ アナザー デイ

BOND   JINX   ZAO   FROST   GRAVES

JAMES BOND. MY CHOICE.

Limited edition

www.omegawatches.com

We don't want to have logos shout out at you. It has to be seamless with the storyline. So, we all work together at making sure that whatever product we choose fits with the plot of the film. We're also very selective with our product placement partners and we have a very unique strategy; we're mainly interested in our partners doing advertising and cross-promotional activities, as opposed to giving us a cheque. There's always been a strong licensing programme around Bond. Today we're actually very broad and the question is how do you develop products within our large consumer group. It's a very wide spectrum that goes from the toy car to video games from Electronic Arts to a very expensive pen or a lighter from ST Dupont. We also realized that yes, men are Bond fans but so are women. Anywhere in the world, over 50 per cent of women say that they are Bond fans, which is a huge number. So over the years, we have developed products for women. We also have been taking product placement to another level in recent years. A classic example is our partnership with Omega; we went to them and said, 'we want the placement and promotion but we also want a licensed product.' So in addition to promoting the Seamaster as James Bond's watch, they also developed a 40th Anniversary Seamaster watch, and produced 10,007 – which sold out in four days. We then went to their parent group, Swatch and developed a line of watches – each one themed after one of the films. And from a placement standpoint, all the watches worn in the film were a Swatch brand. We proved that we can be partners beyond just the release of the film.

The video game strategy was a big step in trying to reach a younger audience. Our *GoldenEye* video game has sold over 8 million copies, it is one of the most successful video games ever. We recently did a *From Russia With Love* video game – it is a Sixties environment based on the original movie, yet it has huge appeal with a younger audience. To me, that really speaks of the strength of the brand across every different age demographic. KEITH SNELGROVE

Die Another Day was the largest premiere we ever organized for a Bond film. We could not get the Odeon Leicester Square, so we did it at the Royal Albert Hall. We did tests to make sure the film could be projected and heard properly, as if we were in a movie theatre.
We dressed the Albert Hall to make it look like icicles were coming down from the ceiling, we had special lights. We had the party in Hyde Park, and a benefit with a poster and stills exhibition for the regular public over the following few days. Since this was the 40th Anniversary, we also had an exhibition at the Science Museum. It was quite amazing.
The day after the premiere, we left for Paris, then Berlin, Sweden...
We opened the film almost at the same time everywhere. ANNE BENNETT

The premiere is the culmination of so many things. It takes two years to make a movie so by the time we get to the premiere, it's a mixture of so many things; but one is the relief that you finally finished the film. You're always hoping that it will meet or exceed expectations. BARBARA BROCCOLI

JAMES BOND IS BACK!

Bond is one of those things that keeps capturing our imagination and you know it allows us to live vicariously through a character that we'd all like to be. And that's unusual in films where you keep boldly sticking with plan time and time again. So what I'm saying is, in general, when you manage to create something as successful as Bond, don't change the plan; keep the plan the way it is, you'll do fine. RIDLEY SCOTT

One of the reasons why I initially got involved with Indiana Jones was because I wanted to do a Bond film. When George Lucas and I were vacationing in Hawaii on the eve of the opening of *Star Wars* in 1977, George asked me what I wanted to do next and I said, 'I want to do a James Bond movie.' And he told me the story of Indiana Jones to prevent me from directing a Bond picture and he put me in his own franchise instead... STEVEN SPIELBERG

When I saw my first Bond films, I wanted to join the secret service. I didn't want to be an architect, a doctor, a fireman or a film-maker any more, I wanted to be a secret agent because that's how you got all the beautiful girls and where you got all the action. I think if I was doing a Bond film, I'd set it in the Sixties. I think it would be very cool to have Bond forever stuck in the mid-Sixties fighting the Soviet Union, or SPECTRE, and living in that era. I want these films to continue as long as I live, I want to see them every two years, I want Barbara Broccoli and Michael Wilson to continue being brave and making them. PETER JACKSON

By the time Cubby was finished with *Dr No*, he was already starting on the next one. He was always confident James Bond would return. We are too. MICHAEL G. WILSON

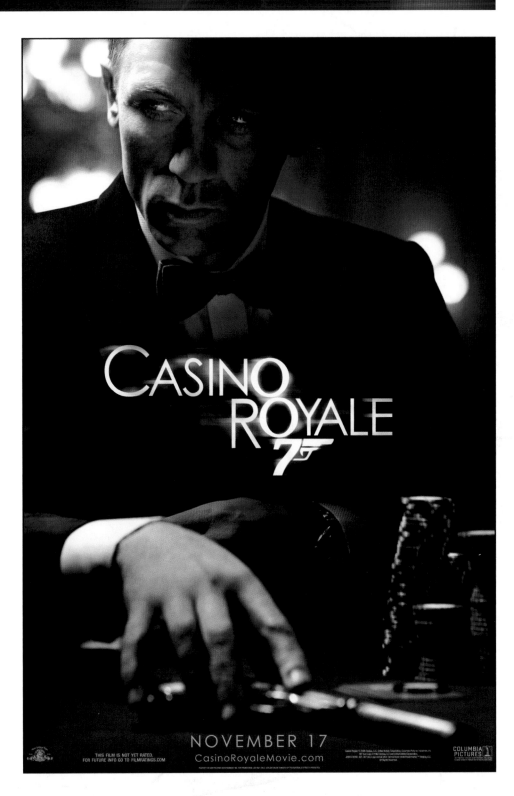

Once the new Bond comes out, we're usually already on to the next one. After all, we end each film with the line 'James Bond Will Return'. BARBARA BROCCOLI

PICTURE CAPTIONS

p4: In 2006 Daniel Craig became the sixth actor to portray James Bond, making his debut in Eon Productions's big-screen adaptation of Ian Fleming's first 007 novel, *Casino Royale*.

p6: A SPECTRE helicopter pursues Bond. Although meant to be set on the outskirts of Hungary, this dramatic sequence in *From Russia With Love* was actually filmed in Scotland, where Sean Connery did much of the stunt work himself.

p7: Drawn by an artist from original studio-posed photos of Sean Connery, this is just one of the many images used on the USA poster art and ad campaign for *From Russia With Love*.

p8: Famed poster artist Bob Peak was commissioned to design a series of teaser posters for the second Timothy Dalton 007 adventure, *Licence to Kill*. However, none were used in the final marketing campaign.

p10: Taken from the original French release poster of *Dr No*, this stunning art by illustrator Boris Grinsson was copied from a press still of Ursula Andress and Sean Connery that originally showed a tattoo on Connery's arm that he had received in the Royal Navy.

p14: Although *Casino Royale* breaks with many traditional elements of the Bond series, one important mainstay is the classic image of 007 at a gambling table dressed in a tuxedo.

p15: Early US covers of Ian Fleming's novels. Although Fleming had built a loyal following for his fiction, the release of the Bond films elevated sales of his books exponentially. Fleming died in 1964 at the age of 56, shortly before the release of *Goldfinger*.

p16: Publicity still of Ian Fleming in Istanbul, during filming for *From Russia With Love*. Fleming had tried unsuccessfully for years to bring the Bond franchise to the screen. In desperation, he sold the screen rights for *Casino Royale* for $1,000 in 1954. This resulted in a one-hour live TV version of the novel broadcast in October of that year on the American network CBS. Ultimately, Fleming decided producers Cubby Broccoli and Harry Saltzman were best qualified to turn his stories into feature films.

p17: To promote its daily comic-strip stories of Ian Fleming's Bond novels, the *Daily Express* newspaper produced this poster for news-stands in and around London. Although published before the films were made, it is interesting to see how artist John McLusky's portrayal of Bond bears an uncanny likeness to that of actor Sean Connery.

p18: Ian Fleming wanted a bland, innocuous name for his literary hero and admitted to 'stealing' the name James Bond from the author of the book *Birds of the West Indies*. Fleming and the real-life James Bond became friends and Mr Bond was an invited guest to Fleming's Jamaican home Goldeneye.

p19: During the filming of *Dr No* in Jamaica, Bond author Ian Fleming (seen here with Ursula Andress) would often visit the set to witness how his novel was being transferred to the cinema screen.

p20: Bond launches a counter-attack against Stromberg's forces in *The Spy Who Loved Me* accompanied by Capt. Carter, played by Shane Rimmer – a popular American character actor who also appeared in *You Only Live Twice* and *Diamonds Are Forever*.

p21: This scene from *Dr No* caused substantial controversy in 1962. Censors objected to the fact that Bond killed Prof. Dent even though the villain's gun was empty – and administered a coup de grace by firing several more shots into Dent as he lay prone. Ultimately, the producers agreed to trim the sequence and reduce the number of shots fired by Bond.

p22: Elektra King (Sophie Marceau) delights in having Bond in a chair especially built for strangulation in *The World Is Not Enough*.

p23: Sean Connery as James Bond, on the set of *Dr No*.

p24: Sean Connery chats with Ian Fleming on location in Jamaica for *Dr No*.

p25: Italian actress Daniela Bianchi was chosen from hundreds of women for the role of Tatiana in *From Russia With Love*.

pp26/27: To film the hijacking of the bombs and the murder of Domino's brother in the sunken Vulcan bomber plane in *Thunderball*, the production crew built a full-scale portion of the plane and sunk it out at sea off Nassau in the Bahamas.

p28: *Top left:* Joseph Wiseman was an acclaimed actor of stage and screen when he accepted the role of Dr No, making history as the first Bond screen villain. Ian Fleming had approached his old friend Noel Coward to play Dr No, but the witty Coward responded by writing 'Dear Ian, the answer to your question about Dr No is…No! No! No!'. It isn't known if Coward ever regretted his decision. *Below right:* Bond fights his way through Dr No's secret complex amidst widespread destruction to save Honey. The scene is yet another example of Ken Adam's innovative production designs for the film that were achieved on a shoestring budget.

p29: This very rare advert for *Dr No* was never used in the film's campaign.

p30: Bond's now-famous golf game with Auric Goldfinger was filmed at Stoke Park, a prestigious private club on the outskirts of London. The house was also utilised in *Tomorrow Never Dies* for the scene in which Bond discovers the body of Paris Carver in a hotel room.

p31: Goldfinger's 1937 Sedanca De Ville Rolls Royce was sold off after filming, and was in private ownership for many years. Today, it is back where it belongs – in the archive of Eon Productions.

pp32/33: Three different quad posters were designed and issued to promote the 1967 film *You Only Live Twice*. Famed American illustrator Robert McGinnis painted this image.

p34: *From Russia With Love*. Bond and Tatiana aboard the Orient Express with SPECTRE assassin Red Grant, posing as MI6 agent Capt. Nash.

p35: In the climax of *Live And Let Die*, Bond utilises a watch with a mini buzz-saw device to prevent being lowered into Kananga's shark pool. However, fans complained that the sequence broke a cardinal rule of Bond lore by not telling the audience in advance of this feature – a strategy not employed by the scriptwriters since. *Inset sketch:* The grotto set was built on D Stage at Pinewood Studios. The elevated cage structure (seen here in an early sketch) was designed by Production Manager Syd Cain.

p36: In 1976, Cubby Broccoli hosted a spectacular opening of the famous 007 Stage at Pinewood Studios. Former Prime Minister Harold Wilson was among the dignitaries attending to kick off production on *The Spy Who Loved Me*.

p37: Bond battles the giant Jaws in *The Spy Who Loved Me*. The villain, played by Richard Kiel, was initially supposed to be a truly menacing figure but Kiel played the role with a touch of humour. The character proved to be so popular he was brought back in the next film, *Moonraker*.

p38: Bond in action in *The World Is Not Enough*. For these explosive sequences, Production Designer Peter Lamont built large-scale, complex sets on the Albert R. Broccoli 007 Stage at Pinewood Studios.

p39: Sophie Marceau as Elektra King, the deceitful femme fatale of *The World Is Not Enough*.

p40: Daniel Craig as James Bond and Eva Green as Vesper Lynd share a tender moment in *Casino Royale*.

p41: Bond takes his chances against brilliant card player Le Chiffre in *Casino Royale*. *Inset:* Preliminary production design sketch for the Casino Royale exterior.

pp42/43: *Left:* The film of *Casino Royale* reproduces one of the most harrowing sequences in Fleming's original novel, as Bond finds himself tied to a chair and tortured by Le Chiffre. *Right:* Preliminary production artwork for the scene.

p44: Roger Moore jokes with Yaphet Kotto, who plays the villain Dr Kananga in *Live And Let Die*. Kotto was a veteran supporting actor who had his most prominent role to date in this 1973 Bond hit.

p45: Roger Moore finds the energy to joke around on the set of *The Spy Who Loved Me* – despite toiling in a tuxedo in the boiling temperatures of the Egyptian desert.

p46: Sean Connery returned to the role of Bond in *Diamonds Are Forever* following a one-picture absence. Lana Wood, sister of actress Natalie Wood, played Plenty O'Toole, an innocent opportunist who pays a heavy price for her dalliance with 007.

p47: Bond engages in a literal dance of death with black widow SPECTRE agent Fiona Volpe (Luciana Paluzzi) at the Kiss-Kiss Club in Nassau. *Inset:* Costume Designer Anthony Mendleson's original sketch for Fiona's dress.

p48: Sean Connery rehearses the Bambi and Thumper fight in *Diamonds Are Forever*.

p49: Distinguished British character actor Charles Gray in *Diamonds Are Forever* was the third man to play SPECTRE chieftain Ernst Stavro Blofeld.

p50: *Left:* Bond turns Jaws's metallic teeth to his advantage by using a magnet to give him an unwanted lift in *The Spy Who Loved Me* – another example of the grandiose sets associated with Ken Adam's production designs. *Inset:* Jaws takes a bite out of a predator in the ultimate 'man-eating shark' joke.

p51: Richard Kiel as Jaws in *The Spy Who Loved Me* – a villain not prone to being in touch with modern sensibilities. Kiel was offered the role of Darth Vader in *Star Wars* but opted to play Jaws in *The Spy Who Loved Me* instead because he felt he could bring more nuances to this character than he could if he were confined behind a black mask.

p52: Honor Blackman as Pussy Galore in *Goldfinger*. Censors argued that the character's suggestive name be changed to Kitty. However, the producers countered that when Prince Phillip had visited the set and met with Blackman, the press had dutifully printed her character's name in the context of the story. Their reasoning prevailed and Pussy Galore became one of the most famous film characters of all time.

p53: Bond goes 'around the world' with Holly Goodhead (Lois Chiles) at the conclusion of *Moonraker*.

pp56/57: Although Ken Adam's most famous set is his SPECTRE volcano for *You Only Live Twice*, the film also featured other outstanding examples of production design such as Blofeld's lair, shown here.

pp58/59: Ken Adam's original sketch for the underground lair set in *Dr No* and *(opposite)* the finished sequence as seen in the film. Adam's futuristic designs for *Dr No* so impressed Stanley Kubrick that he hired Adam to design the famous War Room set for *Dr Strangelove*.

pp60/61: For the room in which Prof. Dent (Anthony Dawson) is given a tarantula with which to kill James Bond, Ken Adam used a minimal set with ingenious lighting effects to simulate a feel of terror and evoke the sense that the room itself was a spider's web. p61, *bottom:* Ken Adam's original sketch for a deleted sequence from *Dr No* in which Bond rescues Honey from being devoured by flesh-eating crabs. When the creatures proved too lethargic to perform, director Terence Young re-shot the sequence showing Honey shackled to the floor as the ocean waters slowly rise around her.

p62: Ken Adam's spectacular set for Fort Knox is the centre of the climactic battle in *Goldfinger*. Adam's universally acclaimed work on the Bond films made him one of the few production designers to become a celebrity in his own right. Incredibly, it would not be until

The Spy Who Loved Me that he would receive an Oscar nomination for his work on a Bond film. He was nominated for Oscars on five occasions, winning for *Barry Lyndon* and *The Madness of King George*.

p63: Seemingly invincible, Oddjob (Harold Sakata) ironically becomes the victim of his own lethal, razor-brimmed bowler hat when Bond uses it as a tool to electrocute him. Sakata, who wrestled under the name Tosh Togo, used his fame as Oddjob to make countless public appearances dressed as the character.

pp64/65: Ken Adam's sketch for the famous *Goldfinger* 'laser-room' scene. The 'beam' of the laser was an optical effect added after filming. However, for the close-ups where the flame cuts through the metal, special-effects technician Bert Luxford was hidden away underneath the table with a blowtorch.

p66: Adolfo Celi as Emilio Largo, SPECTRE's No. 2 agent, at the French HQ hidden away behind the façade of a Paris charity for stateless persons. Again, the genius of Ken Adam is apparent in this futuristic design for *Thunderball* that included an electric chair used to assassinate a corrupt SPECTRE agent.

p67: Ken Adam at work on *Thunderball* and his original production sketch for the SPECTRE boardroom scene.

p68: The impressive volcano set from *You Only Live Twice* cost almost as much to build as the entire budget of the first James Bond film *Dr No*, and was so large it could be seen some three miles away.

p69: Ken Adam's early production sketch for the SPECTRE volcano set.

p70: Original sketch and finished shot of *The Man With The Golden Gun* reactor set. Peter Murton took over as Production Designer on Roger Moore's second Bond film, *The Man With The Golden Gun*. He had previously worked as Art Director with Ken Adam on *Dr Strangelove, Goldfinger, Thunderball* and the first Harry Palmer film, *The Ipcress File*. The illustrations on these pages show that Murton's work on *Golden Gun* was very much in the Ken Adam tradition of large-scale sets with futuristic design qualities.

p71: Scaramanga's deadly maze in the finished film, and one of Murton's sketches of the villain's stylish, sophisticated lair.

p72: The scale and scope of *The Spy Who Loved Me* demanded a set that could contain

two nuclear submarines. When told by Ken Adam that no sound stage in the world was big enough, Cubby Broccoli simply said, 'Build it!' Adam's 007 Stage at Pinewood Studios also hosted many other major productions, including *Superman*.

p73: A closer view of the same set shows the incredible detail provided by Ken Adam – including working elevators and multi-level sets.

p74: Stromberg (Curt Jurgens) toys with his secretary (Marilyn Galsworthy) before dispatching her to a shark tank in *The Spy Who Loved Me*. Inset: A typical Ken Adam dining-room set: opulent backgrounds and boardroom-size tables. These types of characteristics came to define the 'look' of a James Bond movie.

p75: For *The Spy Who Loved Me*, Derek Meddings and his team built a large-scale miniature of Stromberg's underwater city Atlantis and filmed it on location in the shallow waters of the Bahamas.

p76: Drax's underground shuttle launch-pad complex in *Moonraker* was a miniature set complete with lights, moving machinery and vehicles. Built and shot at Pinewood Studios by Derek Meddings, many different scale models of the shuttles, some with engines that actually fired, were utilised for the film. Inset: Preparatory design material for one of the most memorable sequences in *Moonraker*, where James Bond finds himself trapped inside a centrifuge used to acclimatise astronauts to zero-gravity conditions.

p77: An original Ken Adam production design sketch of Drax's hijacked Moonraker shuttle.

p78: A protégé of Ken Adam, Peter Lamont began work on the early Bond films as a draughtsman. Commencing with *For Your Eyes Only*, he has served as Production Designer on most of the 007 films, including *Casino Royale*. Here, Lamont – who won an Oscar for *Titanic* – displays the memorable octopus-style bed he created for *Octopussy*. Inset: Early visualisation artwork of the villainess's lair.

p79: Perhaps the last of the legendary Hollywood producers and showmen, Cubby Broccoli was a larger-than-life presence in the film industry and received every conceivable honour, including tributes from heads of state. Prior to the Bond films, he was also a successful producer in partnership with Irving Allen, with whom he formed Warwick Films. Although American by birth, Cubby enjoyed making the majority of his films in England.

p80: The St Petersburg tank-chase sequence for *GoldenEye* was one of the most ambitious action scenes ever staged for a Bond film. Here, Pierce Brosnan is seen in the final sequence. To the left are original production storyboards.

p81: A classic example of how closely the film crew follow the original storyboards. Production Designer Peter Lamont recreated the streets of St Petersburg down to the smallest detail.

p82: Original sketches of Carver's evasive Stealth Ship in *Tomorrow Never Dies*, designed by Allan Cameron. John Richardson built the final miniature version and filmed it in Mexico.

p83: The Bond production designs have generally utilised contemporary technology as evidenced by this sequence from *Tomorrow Never Dies* in which Carver (Jonathan Pryce) uses the technological capabilities of his media empire for nefarious purposes.

p84: The caviar factory set in *The World Is Not Enough* was originally supposed to be an abandoned oil terminal. Built at Pinewood Studios, Production Designer Peter Lamont had the outdoor tank extended by almost a third of its original length. He had 80ft-high black painted backdrops erected on all sides, totally encapsulating the set so it could be filmed in a panoramic 360 degrees.

p85: The highly dangerous nature of the helicopter attack on Bond at the caviar factory required intricate storyboarding for both the director and SFX team to work from.

pp86/87: Maquette and design sketch of one of the most visually stunning sets ever created for a Bond film, the Ice Palace in *Die Another Day*. The interior was built on the 007 Stage at Pinewood Studios with a large portion of the exterior created on the back lot. p87 shows the final illusion.

p88: A section of Venice, complete with canals, was built in miniature on the Pinewood Studios exterior water tank for the key 'sinking house' sequence in *Casino Royale*.

p89: Early visualisation artwork of the Venetian 'sinking house' sequence in *Casino Royale*.

p90: Largo's home in *Thunderball* is in reality a privately owned property on the exclusive beachfront area of Paradise Island in the Bahamas. Inset: A production drawing of the house's exterior.

THE ART OF BOND

p91: James Bond and Vesper Lynd take a boat trip down Venice's Grand Canal in *Casino Royale*.

p92: The helicopter pad at the Schilthorn mountaintop restaurant used as Blofeld's HQ in *On Her Majesty's Secret Service*. *Inset:* George Lazenby with Blofeld's 'Angels of Death' in the rotating room that serves as the restaurant 'Piz Gloria'. The site, accessible only by cable car, remains a major tourist attraction in Switzerland.

p93: Posed publicity shot of Sean Connery on the Vegas Strip for *Diamonds Are Forever*. *Inset:* The film featured a spectacular car chase between Bond's Mustang and local police officers amidst the glitter of the famed casinos.

pp94/95: The talents of American illustrator Robert McGinnis were employed for the impressive artwork for the *Live And Let Die* poster campaigns around the world.

p96: Roger Moore at the entrance to Ross Kananga's crocodile farm in Jamaica, where scenes for Moore's debut Bond film *Live And Let Die* were filmed.

p97: The producers were so grateful to Ross Kananga for providing the crocodiles and for performing the death-defying stunt in which Bond runs across the backs of the deadly animals, that they named the villain of the story Dr Kananga in his honour. The stunt was achieved by strapping the crocodiles down but Kananga still came perilously close to being injured during numerous takes.

p98: For the destruction of Scaramanga's island during the climax of *The Man With The Golden Gun*, Derek Meddings constructed a huge model on the Pinewood exterior tank of the real-life location situated in Phuket, Thailand.

p99: M's office in *The Man With The Golden Gun* was hidden away in the half-sunken wreckage of the Queen Mary in Hong Kong's harbour. Production Designer Peter Murton came up with the outlandish idea of the crooked levels within the ship (*see sketch below*) and these were replicated on sets at Pinewood.

p100: Built at Leavesden studios in England, this model of the satellite dish as seen in *GoldenEye* was capable of filling with water in several minutes (see overflow tank in background) and was one of the largest miniatures built for a Bond film.

p101: A villain's demise – Bond style. The climax of *GoldenEye* saw Bond and

Trevelyan in a fight to the death atop the satellite dish at Arecibo.

p102: Pierce Brosnan with Michelle Yeoh as fellow covert operator Wai Lin in *Tomorrow Never Dies*. Yeoh exemplified the modern vision of the Bond woman: courageous, intelligent and self-reliant.

P103: Lake Como, northern Italy, provides one of many exotic locations for the film *Casino Royale*.

p104: Storyboard sequence featuring autogiro 'Little Nellie' in *You Only Live Twice*. *Inset:* A frame from the finished scene.

p105: One of the first gadgets introduced in the Bond series was the pair of shoes worn by the villainess Rosa Klebb in *From Russia With Love*. Clicking the shoes together enabled a razor-sharp blade to protrude. It was coated with fast-acting poison that brought death in seconds. Long-time Bond special-effects man Burt Luxford built the shoes.

p106: Iconic British actor Christopher Lee played the villain Scaramanga in *The Man With The Golden Gun*. The ingenious Golden Gun was assembled from common items such as a cigarette lighter and case and a fountain pen. It fired only a single golden bullet, but Scaramanga prided himself on never needing more than one shot. The famous weapon was the creation of special-effects wizard John Stears.

p107: Director Guy Hamilton arranges to shoot a key sequence with Christopher Lee as Scaramanga. *Inset:* The film's American teaser poster showed how the gun was assembled.

p108: Bond pauses for a rare nostalgic moment with Q in *Die Another Day* – the film that marked the 40th anniversary of the first James Bond film, *Dr No*.

p109: The original jetpack in *Thunderball* was loaned by the US Army and flown by engineer Bill Suitor, one of only two men in the world qualified to fly the device. For close-up scenes with Sean Connery (*inset*), a mock-up of the jetpack was built, as evidenced by these schematic drawings.

p110: The only star that threatened to eclipse the actor playing James Bond was the Aston Martin DB5. Introduced in *Goldfinger*, the gadget-laden automobile became an international sensation. Four cars were built for the film, two of which are seen on screen, the other two for promotional purposes. Modified by John Stears, the car featured such

'optional extras' as concealed machines guns, bullet-proof shield, tyre-slashers and the now-famous ejector seat.

p111: Steven Spielberg with his Aston Martin DB9, photographed especially for *The Art of Bond* by Miranda Penn Turin.

p112: Almost as famous as Bond's DB5 was his Lotus Esprit from *The Spy Who Loved Me*. The amazing vehicle was capable of amphibious travel – an effect enacted by having a shell of the car pulled along by a line and steered by a scuba diver inside.

p113: Original production sketches for the Lotus Esprit. Like the Aston Martin DB5, the vehicle was an immediate sensation with the public and was utilised on publicity tours for the movie.

pp114/115: A highlight of *Tomorrow Never Dies* is Bond's nerve-wracking race through a car park whilst controlling his BMW from the back seat via remote control. The original storyboards for the sequence, shown on p115, display the hidden missile rack lodged in the car's sunroof.

p116: Production storyboards for the elaborate ice-chase sequence from *Die Another Day*. On the early films, storyboards were drawn in pencil and never colorized.

p117: Whilst the majority of the car chase on ice was filmed in Iceland, some special effects and close-ups were filmed on location in the UK. *Inset:* The fiery trail of a missile launched from Zao's Jaguar was added in post-production, using CGI.

pp118/119: Continuing a grand tradition, Bond is seen behind the wheel of an Aston Martin DB5 in *Casino Royale*. *Inset:* Bond mixes the old with the new, alternating the classic DB5 with the new Aston Martin DBS. The long association between Eon Productions and Aston Martin extends back to *Goldfinger*.

p122: *The Man With The Golden Gun* featured the first movie stunt to be devised with the use of a computer. The sequence in which Bond's AMC Hornet makes a 360-degree spin over a canal bridge was calculated by Jay Milligan (2nd from left). Here Roger Moore, Milligan, Cubby Broccoli and the crew celebrate the success of the spectacular stunt.

p123: Cubby Broccoli and Harry Saltzman in the South Audley Street offices of Eon, circa mid 1960s.

p124: Director Terence Young taking a break on the set of *From Russia With Love* with Daniela Bianchi in Istanbul. Young was pivotal to the success of the early Bond films, having also directed the first release, *Dr No*. He returned to the franchise for the last time with *Thunderball* in 1965.

p125: Cubby Broccoli and Sean Connery relax between takes whilst filming *Dr No* in Jamaica. It was Cubby's wife Dana who first suggested hiring Connery for the role of Bond, having been impressed by his charisma in the Disney film *Darby O'Gill and the Little People*.

pp126/127: Live and Let Dine: A master of innovation, Cubby Broccoli personally prepared meals for the cast and crew when catering problems arose on the set of *The Spy Who Loved Me*. Roger Moore gives a willing assist.

p128: Early in the filming of *Dr No*, director Terence Young rehearses a scene with Sean Connery and Reggie Carter, who plays the double agent posing as Bond's chauffeur in Jamaica.

p129: Director Guy Hamilton rehearsing the golf sequence at Stoke Park for *Goldfinger*. Observing his technique is Cubby Broccoli, Gert Frobe and Harold Sakata (in background).

p130: Cubby and Harry discuss strategies on location in Jamaica for *Dr No*. Although the two envisioned creating a series, Cubby later confessed that neither man foresaw the longevity of the Bond films.

p131: Sean Connery relaxes between takes on the set of *Dr No*.

p132: Producer Michael G. Wilson with his son David, on the set of *Casino Royale*. *Inset:* Oscar-winning costume designer Lindy Hemming at work on *Casino Royale*.

p133: New Zealander Lee Tamahori directs a complex sequence for *Die Another Day*.

p134: The train fight between Bond and Red Grant (Robert Shaw) in *From Russia With Love* is considered to be one of the best-directed and best-edited action sequences ever filmed. The actors did most of their own stunts after studying Greco-Roman wrestling techniques.

p135: A full decade after directing the smash hit *GoldenEye*, Martin Campbell returns to the franchise for *Casino Royale*. His films in the interim include *The Mask of Zorro, Beyond Borders* and *The Legend of Zorro*.

p136: Rare photo from Pierce Brosnan's screentest for the part of James Bond.

p137: Connery rehearsing the bedroom scene with Daniela Bianchi for *From Russia With Love*.

p138: Sean Connery relaxing between takes for the Orient Express sequence in *From Russia With Love*. The record-breaking grosses for the film would launch Connery into superstar status.

p139: Sean Connery enjoys some of the finer things in life in *Goldfinger*.

pp140/141: Australian actor George Lazenby, the second man to play James Bond on screen, on the set of *On Her Majesty's Secret Service*.

p142: Roger Moore and Gloria Hendry (as double agent Rosie Carver) in *Live and Let Die*.

p143: Already an established star of films and television, Roger Moore assumed the role of James Bond in *Live And Let Die*.

p144: Timothy Dalton became the fourth actor to play Bond with *The Living Daylights*. This pose was used on the film's teaser poster and emphasised the dramatic aspects that Dalton brought to the role.

p145: Dalton enjoying a laugh with leading lady Maryam d'Abo on the set of *The Living Daylights*.

p146: Pierce Brosnan receiving direction from Lee Tamahori on the set of *Die Another Day*. The film would prove to be the top grossing entry in the series up to that date.

p147: Pierce Brosnan in his debut as 007 at the Monte Carlo Casino in *GoldenEye*. Exteriors for the scene were actually filmed in Monte Carlo, but the interior sequences were shot at Leavesden Studios on the outskirts of London. The entire studio was built inside an old aircraft factory especially for this film and would later host other major productions such as the *Star Wars* franchise.

p148: Daniel Craig is James Bond in *Casino Royale*.

p149: James Bond, played by Daniel Craig, in the Casino Royale.

p150: The Bond films have long attracted top talent in all fields. Diana Rigg had the pivotal role of Tracy, the fiercely independent Italian countess who marries 007 in *On Her Majesty's*

Secret Service – albeit with tragic results. Rigg, already a popular star of TV's *The Avengers*, was inspired to do the film because she had never been in an 'epic'.

p151: Ursula Andress set the standard for all of the Bond women who followed her. Her emergence from the sea in a white bikini in *Dr No* is still one of the great screen entrances.

p152: Honor Blackman as Pussy Galore in the barn sequence for *Goldfinger*.

p153: Publicity shot of Gloria Hendry as Rosie Carver in *Live And Let Die*.

p154: The stunning French actress Carole Bouquet *(For Your Eyes Only)* also had a successful career as a top fashion model. For years, she represented Chanel in the company's international advertising campaigns.

p155: Born in America, Barbara Bach subsequently emigrated to Italy, where she worked as a fashion model before entering the acting profession.

p156: James Bond (Pierce Brosnan) tangles with the deadly Xenia Onatopp (Famke Janssen) in *GoldenEye*.

p157: Sophie Marceau as Elektra King in *The World Is Not Enough*. *Inset:* Lindy Hemming's original sketch for Elektra's stunning evening dress.

p158: Halle Berry was already signed for the role of Jinx for *Die Another Day* when she was awarded the Best Actress Oscar for *Monster's Ball*.

p159: Rosamund Pike as the beautiful but duplicitous MI6 agent Miranda Frost in *Die Another Day*.

pp160/161: Halle Berry's rise from the surf in *Die Another Day* was an intentional homage to Ursula Andress's first screen appearance in *Dr No* forty years previously.

p162: Catarina Murino, a former Miss Italy, plays the role of Solange in *Casino Royale*.

p163: French actress Eva Green as Vesper Lynd in *Casino Royale*. Her previous film credits include Ridley Scott's *Kingdom of Heaven* and Bernardo Bertolucci's *The Dreamers*.

p164: Acclaimed German actor Gert Frobe in his immortal performance as Auric Goldfinger.

p165: Bond's first encounter with Oddjob, the mute Korean henchman of Auric Goldfinger. The sequence was set in a suite at the Fontainbleau Hotel in Miami but was actually shot at Pinewood Studios.

p166: Veteran British actor Donald Pleasence exudes menace as Blofeld in *You Only Live Twice*.

p167: Charles Gray as the arch-villain Blofeld in *Diamonds Are Forever*.

p168: One of the most prominent actors to emerge from post-war Germany, Curt Jurgens made the transition to English-language films and became a popular international star. Prior to starring as Stromberg in *The Spy Who Loved Me*, Jurgens had won two BAFTA nominations for *The Inn of the Sixth Happiness* and *The Enemy Below*.

p169: Richard Kiel may be known as one of the cinema's great tough guys but he concedes he was almost done in by the metallic teeth he had to wear in his scenes as Jaws in *The Spy Who Loved Me (top right)* and *Moonraker (below)*. The dental fixture was excruciatingly painful and Kiel could only keep it in his mouth for very short periods.

p170: When James Bond returned to the big screen after a six-year absence in *GoldenEye*, he was a more realistic and cynical character who has to deal with questions about his relevance in the post-Cold War environment. He must also contend with the betrayal of his trusted colleague Alec Trevelyan (Sean Bean).

p171: The crew prepare the set for Bond's spectacular rooftop escape in *Tomorrow Never Dies*.

p172: CGI was used in post-production to create this hologram of a bullet lodged in Renard's brain in *The World Is Not Enough*.

p173: A consistent theme in the Bond series is that 007 must confront exotic, highly sophisticated enemies. In *Die Another Day* these include the charismatic Gustav Graves (Toby Stevens) and his henchman Zao (Rick Yune).

p174: The character of Le Chiffre has special resonance to the 007 legacy: he is literally the very first Bond villain. Mads Mikkelsen plays the role in the first truly legitimate screen version of Fleming's first Bond novel.

p175: Sebastien Foucan – a gifted exponent of 'parkour' (otherwise known as 'free-running') – as the villainous Mollaka. *Casino Royale* marks Foucan's first role in a major feature film.

p176: Desmond Llewelyn made his first screen appearance as the gadget master 'Q' in *From Russia With Love*, following Peter Burton, who introduced the character in *Dr No*. Shown here *(from top, clockwise)* in *The World Is Not Enough*, *Licence To Kill* and during the making of *For Your Eyes Only*, Llewelyn is the only cast member of the series to appear opposite the first five Bond actors.

p177: Although Miss Moneypenny generally gets limited screen time, the character is beloved by all fans and the nature of her relationship with Bond has been left intentionally opaque. Lois Maxwell (above in *From Russia With Love* and below in *Goldfinger*) played the character up to and including *A View To A Kill*.

pp178/179: With the introduction of Pierce Brosnan as 007 in *GoldenEye*, Samantha Bond (left in *The World Is Not Enough* and opposite in *Die Another Day*) played a Moneypenny for the 90s; independent, headstrong and quite capable of matching Bond double entendre for double entendre.

p180: Bond's relationship with his superior 'M' is a key ingredient to the series. Although occasionally the atmosphere between them becomes strained and abrasive, there is a deep, if unspoken, mutual respect. Acclaimed British character actor Bernard Lee played the role up to and including *Moonraker* and was succeeded by Robert Brown. *Main picture:* An imaginative link to a previous era is seen in *The World Is Not Enough* – an oil painting of Bernard Lee adorns the office of the new 'M', Judi Dench.

p181: Fans were sceptical of having a female 'M' – until they saw the hard-edged performance given by Judi Dench in her first on-screen appearance opposite Pierce Brosnan in *GoldenEye*. One of England's most acclaimed actresses, Dame Judi's no-nonsense approach to the part earned her immediate respect from both critics and the public.

pp182/183: Every Bond film has featured a pre-credits sequence except the first, *Dr No*. In many cases, these spectacular openings have nothing to do with the main plot that follows, but in the case of *Casino Royale*, the scenes are pivotal to establishing the character of James Bond.

p184: Director Peter Hunt filmed the pre-credits beach fight in *On Her Majesty's Secret Service* in Portugal. The brilliantly staged and edited sequence took full advantage of new Bond George Lazenby's exceptional athletic prowess.

p185: A rare original prop from *You Only Live Twice* – the Hong Kong newspaper that reports Bond's 'death'. Note the attention to detail: although the paper is only glimpsed fleetingly onscreen, the full story is actually written out.

pp186/187: The famous ski jump in *The Spy Who Loved Me* was inspired by an advertisement for Canadian Club whisky.

pp188/189: The spectacular pre-credits sequence of *Tomorrow Never Dies* opens with Bond causing mayhem at a terrorist arms-bazaar. Here are the original storyboards depicting how the scene should be filmed, opposite the finished scene.

p190: Original production sketches for the 'Q' boat in action on the River Thames in London. Second Unit Director Vic Armstrong co-ordinated and filmed this amazing action sequence.

p191: 'Cigar Girl' (Maria Grazia Cucinotta) almost bests 007 from a hot-air balloon that hovers over London's Millenium Dome in *The World Is Not Enough*. The scene, which finds 007 wounded when plunging from the balloon, followed the Thames boat chase.

pp192/193: Bond 'greets' the widow of SPECTRE assassin Jacques Boitier – and exposes him to be the man himself. Bob Simmons, a long-time stuntman and fight-scene co-ordinator on the Bond films, played the not so fair 'lady'.

p194: In order to assist Roger Moore in mastering the art of driving a London double-decker bus in *Live And Let Die*, Eon hired Maurice Patchett to tutor the actor. Patchett was well qualified – he taught safety driving procedures to actual London bus drivers.

p195: The famous car chase sequence from *Diamonds Are Forever*.

p196: Geoffrey Holder, who portrays the evil Baron Samedi in *Live And Let Die*, is primarily known for being an internationally acclaimed stage director, choreographer and costume designer.

p197: One of the most impressive car stunts in any Bond film, Bond's spectacular jump over a Thai canal in *The Man With The Golden Gun*. The highly dangerous stunt was performed by 'Bumps' Willard in one take.

pp198/199: *Left:* Original storyboards of the complicated sequence in which a helicopter pursues Bond and Wai Lin through a densely populated urban area. The scene was the

brainchild of writer Bruce Feirstein, who said he simply thought it would be fun to create a scene in which a motorcycle somehow soared over the top of a helicopter. *Right:* The finished sequence as it appears in *Tomorrow Never Dies*.

pp200/201: *Left:* Pierce Brosnan and Michelle Yeoh make a death-defying escape in *Tomorrow Never Dies*, using a giant poster of Elliot Carver to break their fall. *Right:* Original storyboards for the same sequence.

pp202/203: Mollaka (Sebastien Foucan), a villain with an almost super-human athletic ability, is pursued by Bond across a construction site in a thrilling 'free-running' chase scene from *Casino Royale*.

p206: John Barry's contributions to the success of the Bond films cannot be over-stated. The Oscar-winning composer is seen here at the London premiere of *Goldfinger*, 1964.

p207: John Barry conducting one of his most inspired Bond scores, *You Only Live Twice* at CTS Studios in London, 1967.

p208: An original flyer issued by EMI Music Ltd in 1964 to promote the *Goldfinger* soundtrack long-playing record. In America the soundtrack even beat the Beatles to the top of the charts.

p209: Variations of the *Goldfinger* title song were issued throughout the world – all of them using the iconic image of actress Shirley Eaton painted in gold, which was instantly identifiable with James Bond. Shirley Bassey (bottom right) is the only artist to have sung three songs from the series: 'Goldfinger', 'Diamonds Are Forever' and 'Moonraker'.

p210: One of John Barry's finest James Bond scores, *On Her Majesty's Secret Service* took the unusual step of not having a main title song, but an instrumental theme instead.

p211: Director Peter Hunt initially planned to end *On Her Majesty's Secret Service* with the marriage of Bond and Tracy, and then show her murder as the pre-credits sequence in the following film. However, when George Lazenby announced he would only do one film, Hunt had to end the movie with the death scene.

p212: Main Title Designer Maurice Binder with Sheena Easton whilst filming the titles for *For Your Eyes Only*.

p213: Sheena Easton was the first and only performer to actually appear in the titles of a James Bond film whilst singing the song. When the song was nominated for an Academy

Award, Easton performed it on Oscar night as part of a major James Bond production number.

p214: An original David Arnold score from *The World Is Not Enough*.

p215: Pierce Brosnan as Bond and Sophie Marceau as Elektra in *The World Is Not Enough*.

p216: The actor who appeared inside the legendary gun barrel in the first three films was actually stuntman Bob Simmons. Sean Connery did not appear in this iconic opening scene until *Thunderball*, when the scene had to be re-filmed for the Panavision process.

p217: Maurice Binder was a legend in the film industry. His titles for the Bond films became a signature of the series and the tradition continues with his successors. Binder was approached to do the titles for *Dr No* after Cubby Broccoli had been impressed with his main titles for the Cary Grant comedy *The Grass is Greener*.

p218: Although *Dr No* and *From Russia With Love* had both been international box-office hits, it was not until the release of *Goldfinger* that James Bond became a pop-culture phenomenon. The film found the perfect blend of action, spectacle and humour – all encapsulated in the stunning main titles.

p219: Margaret Nolan not only appeared in the titles for *Goldfinger* but was also used in the advertising campaign's posters, and on LP covers. She also had a bit part as Dink in the Miami sequence.

p220: A montage of images from the titles of *GoldenEye* (top left and bottom right) and *Die Another Day* show the tremendous creativity of the series's designers, while remaining faithful to the look established by Binder.

p221: For the main titles of *A View To A Kill*, Maurice Binder employed neon lights to create a unique graphic look.

p224: The Bond films were among the first major movies to utilize high-profile promotional tie-ins with major consumer companies. This series of rare German teaser posters for *The Spy Who Loved Me* promote not only the film, but the Seiko watch Bond wears on screen.

p225: Sean Connery and Honor Blackman aboard the arch-villain's private jet in *Goldfinger*.
p226: Connery's classic pose for the promotion of *From Russia With Love*, using photographer David Hurn's own air pistol – a Walther, incidentally – that he had in the boot of his car.

p228: Eon Senior Vice President of Marketing Anne Bennett consults with producer Michael G. Wilson on the set of *Casino Royale*. Marketing a Bond film is a complicated process that starts well before the cameras begin turning – and continues after the film has premiered.

p229: This unique ad campaign for *Die Another Day* was created exclusively for the Japanese market, where Bond has always enjoyed spectacular success.

p230: With *Casino Royale*, the producers continue their long and successful cross-promotional tie-in with Omega watches. Eon is highly selective about its merchandising partners and always insures that they reinforce Bond's image as a man of high style and sophistication.

p231: The ST Dupont limited edition James Bond boxed lighter set represents the more upscale approach to licensed products that Eon has concentrated on in recent years. Product offshoots and merchandising were virtually after-thoughts on the first few Bond movies. However, by the release of *Thunderball* in 1965, the producers had created the most successful licensing campaign in the history of cinema.

pp232/233: The premiere of *Die Another Day* at London's Royal Albert Hall was the social event of the season. The evening not only celebrated the latest Bond film but also the 40th anniversary of the film franchise. Guests included dozens of cast- and crewmembers from previous movies, including four Bond actors: Roger Moore, George Lazenby, Timothy Dalton and Pierce Brosnan. The screening, attended by Queen Elizabeth II, preceded a spectacular party that replicated the Ice Palace seen in the film.

p234: This Double Crown poster was used on London buses and in cinemas during the launch of *Dr No* in England. The early artwork of the gun and bullets against the 007 prefix was created before the now famous 007 gun-barrel logo became an internationally recognised part of Bond folklore. It also appeared on the James Bond Pan paperback novels of the day.

p235: Official teaser poster for *Casino Royale*.